P9-BZO-761

READ IT AGAIN!

Pre-K
Introducing Literature to Young Children

Discarded by
Westfield Washington
Public Library

WESTFIELD PUBLIC LIBRARY
333 West Hoover Street
Westfield. IN 46074

READ IT AGAIN!

Pre-K
Introducing Literature to Young Children

Libby Miller
Liz Rothlein

Illustrated by Libby Miller

WESTFIELD PUBLIC LIBRARY
333 West Hoover Street
Westfield, IN 46074

GoodYearBooks
An Imprint of ScottForesman
A Division of HarperCollinsPublishers

Good Year Books

are available for preschool through grade 6 for every basic curriculum subject plus many enrichment areas. For more Good Year Books, contact your local bookseller or educational dealer. For a complete catalog with information about other Good Year Books, please write:

Good Year Books
Scott, Foresman and Company
1900 East Lake Avenue
Glenview, Illinois 60025

Copyright © 1992 Libby Miller and Liz Rothlein.
All Rights Reserved.
Printed in the United States of America.

ISBN 0-673-36008-3

4 5 6 7 8 9 MAL 99 98 97 96 95 94

Only portions of this book intended for classroom use may be reproduced without permission in writing from the publisher.

This book is dedicated to my family—Bill, Kymberli, and Ashley—for their confidence, support, and encouragement.—L.M.

To Terri, my beloved daughter and true friend, who I so thoroughly enjoy and respect as a person and as an esteemed educator. May she always remain the beautiful person she is today.—L.R.

CONTENTS

Introduction | viii
Rationale | viii
Objectives | ix
Features | ix
Guidelines for Using This Book | x
References | xii

Selected Books and Activities

INTRODUCTION

Rationale

Our review of current literature on teaching reading has made it clear that using children's books to teach reading is gaining in popularity. For example, Bernice E. Cullinan (1987), former International Reading Association president, has spoken out on the power of trade books to overcome *aliteracy*, a term used for those who can read but don't or won't read. William Bennett (1986), former U.S. Secretary of Education, recommended using more trade books in the elementary classroom as a way to overcome "the deadening quality of what children are given to read." Bill Honig, State Superintendent of Public Education, implemented the California Reading Initiative Program, which consists of curriculum guidebooks to accompany over a thousand trade books recommended for the classroom. The interest in increasing the use of trade books in an attempt to overcome illiteracy in the United States is mounting. Most recently, First Lady Barbara Bush announced the formation of the Barbara Bush Foundation for Family Literacy, which will give grants to programs that focus on the family as a key to a more literate nation.

One primary motivation for integrating trade books into the curriculum is that research has repeatedly shown that there is no better way to teach children to read than to read to them and with them (Doake, 1979; Durkin, 1966; Holdaway, 1979; International Reading Association, 1986a, 1986b; Schickedanz, 1983, 1986). In addition to learning to read, children develop personal preferences and special interests in books through this early exposure to literature and are thereby motivated to read books of their own choice. Proponents of literature-based reading programs agree that the success of a reading program should be measured in terms of the number of students who eventually establish the habit of reading for independent learning, personal pleasure, and continued growth.

The attitudes children develop toward reading are also of great importance. As Bruno Bettelheim (1981) so poignantly stated, "A child's attitude toward reading is of such importance that, more often than not, it determines his scholastic fate. Moreover, his experience in learning to read may decide how he will feel about learning in general, and even about himself as a person." Ulrich Hardt (1983) has supported this view, saying, "Children will become readers only if their emotions have been engaged, their imaginations stirred and stretched by what they find on printed pages. One sure way to make this happen is through literature." Therefore, it is important that teachers are trained in methods and techniques for integrating literature into the curriculum and are provided with the appropriate materials.

Many publishers are responding to this call for integrating trade books into the curriculum by publishing guidebooks and kits to aid teachers. *Read It Again! Pre–K* provides the teacher with imaginative teaching ideas for use with eight easily accessible, popular, quality children's books. Children in preschool through grade one will benefit from the materials in this book as they develop a love of reading and thinking. The activities emphasize the interactive process of speaking, listening, reading, and writing, They involve the children in music, art, process writing, cooking, geography, and poetry. The discussion questions suggested for each book reflect the taxonomy developed by B. S. Bloom and others (1956) and focus on developing higher-order thinking skills, requiring the children to analyze, synthesize, and evaluate.

Read It Again! Pre–K can be adapted to almost any classroom setting. The activities can be presented to either large or small groups, are designed for different levels of ability, and can be used to encourage independent work.

Read It Again! Pre–K is also an excellent resource for parents. At-home activities are provided for each of the eight books presented. The suggested books and activities will help parents develop in their children an appreciation for literature and reading and the skills to become effective and involved readers.

Objectives

Read It Again! Pre–K is designed to enable children to develop vital thinking and learning skills. By completing the activities, the children will meet the following objectives developed by the National Council of Teachers of English (1983):

- Realize the importance of literature as a mirror of human experience, reflecting human motives, conflicts, and values.
- Be able to identify with fictional characters in human situations as a means of relating to others; gain insights from involvement with literature.
- Become aware of important writers representing diverse backgrounds and traditions in literature.
- Become familiar with masterpieces of literature, both past and present.
- Develop effective ways of talking and writing about varied forms of literature.
- Experience literature as a way to appreciate the rhythms and beauty of the language.
- Develop habits of reading that carry over into adult life.

Features

Read It Again! Pre–K focuses on eight easy-to-find books. These books have a proven track record of success with children. Many of them are Newbery or Caldecott award winners.

Brown Bear, Brown Bear, What Do You See? by Bill Martin, Jr.
The Carrot Seed by Ruth Krauss
Do You Want to Be My Friend? by Eric Carle
Goodnight Moon by Margaret Wise Brown
Here Are My Hands by Bill Martin, Jr., and John Archambault
If You Give a Mouse a Cookie by Laura Joffe Numeroff
Where's Spot? by Eric Hill
Whose Mouse Are You? by Robert Kraus

Basic information is provided for each book: author, illustrator, publisher and publication date, number of pages, and a list of other works by the same author. This information is followed by a summary of the book and an introduction to use when presenting the book to children. Discussion questions, designed to foster higher-level thinking skills, are then provided. An oral language activity designed to develop vocabulary and concepts is also presented.

One major feature of this book is the large number of activities provided through learning centers, parent bulletins, and additional activities. All of these activities can easily be correlated with basic objectives in language arts, literature, and the social sciences. Many of the activities require worksheets, which are designed to be reproducible.

The learning center section consists of a center activity marker that can be adhered to a piece of cardboard and then stapled to a dowel rod or a stick, which is then placed in a flowerpot. This marker can be changed as each new center activity is introduced, or several flowerpots can be made to allow several centers to operate concurrently. A list of materials needed for use at the centers is provided along with directions for completing the activity.

The parent bulletin is designed to be duplicated and sent home with each child. It provides information about the book being used plus activities parents can do at home that will reinforce the activities at school.

Another major feature is the evaluation sheet provided for each book. This worksheet helps the teacher gain information about what each child has learned from the activities provided.

In addition to these features, other activities and ideas are provided. Some activities are designed for group or individual participation based on the ability and interests of the child. Teachers and parents can determine which activities are most appropriate to meet each child's needs.

Guidelines for Using This Book

Before using the activities in *Read It Again! Pre–K*, it is important that the teacher or parent present the selected books in an interesting and meaningful way. It is imperative that the children enjoy themselves, as well as develop skills that will benefit them as they read on their own. An excellent way to present books to children is by reading them aloud. When reading aloud, the following suggestions may be helpful:

1. Establish a regular schedule for reading aloud.
2. Practice reading the book to acquaint yourself with the story's concepts in advance.
3. Have a prereading session to set the stage for reading the book. Include the title and author/illustrator of the book, an introduction or purpose for listening to the story, an introduction of key vocabulary words, and a discussion about the main parts of the book, such as the book jacket, end pages, author information, and so on.
4. Create a comfortable atmosphere with minimal distraction.
5. Read with feeling and expression. If the spoken dialogue is to sound like conversation, you need to pay careful attention to pitch and stress.
6. When appropriate, hold the book so that everyone can see the print as well as the illustrations.
7. Allow the children to participate in the story when appropriate. Occasionally, you may want to stop and ask the children what they think might happen next or how the story might end.
8. Provide opportunities to respond to the story. Although it is not necessary for the children to respond to every story that is read, they can benefit from such follow-up activities as discussion questions, dramatizations, art activities, book reports, and so on.

The flexible format of *Read It Again! Pre–K* allows the teacher or parent to use it in a variety of ways. The selected books and many of the activities can be presented in any order, although the following format is suggested:

1. Introduce the selected book.
2. Introduce the story-specific vocabulary words.
3. Read the book aloud, or provide enough individual copies of the book and time for the children to read and reread the book.
4. Ask the discussion questions.
5. Introduce the oral language activity.
6. Set up and introduce the learning center activity.
7. Send home the parent bulletin.
8. Do appropriate additional activities/ideas.
9. Initiate the evaluation.

The amount of time allotted to each book will depend on several factors, including the children's age and grade level and flexibility of time and scheduling.

References

Bennett, William J. *First Lessons: A Report on Elementary Education in America.* Washington, D.C.: U.S. Government Printing Office, 1986.

Bettelheim, Bruno. "Attitudes Toward Reading." *Atlantic Monthly*, Nov. 1981, p. 25.

Bloom, B. S., M. B. Englehart, S. J. Furst, W. H. Hill, and D. R. Krathwohl. *Taxonomy of Educational Objectives. The Classification of Educational Goals. Handbook I: Cognitive Domain.* New York: Longmans Green, 1956.

Cullinan, Bernice E. "Books in the Classroom." *The Horn Book*, Nov/Dec. 1986, vol. 62, pp. 766–768.

Cullinan, Bernice E. (ed.). *Children's Literature in the Reading Program.* Newark, Del.: International Reading Association, 1987.

Doake, David. "Book Experience and Emergent Reading Behavior." Paper presented at Preconvention Institute No. 24, Research on Written Language Development, International Reading Association annual convention, Atlanta, April 1979.

Durkin, Dolores. *Children Who Read Early.* New York: Teachers' College Press, 1966.

Hardt, Ulrich. *Teaching Reading with the Other Language Arts.* Newark, Del.: International Reading Association, 1983, p. 108.

Holdaway, Don. *The Foundations of Literacy.* Toronto: Ashton Scholastic, 1979.

International Reading Association. "IRA Position Statement on Reading and Writing in Early Childhood." *The Reading Teacher*, Oct. 1986a, vol. 39, pp. 822–824.

International Reading Association. "Literacy Development and Pre-First Grade: A Joint Statement of Concerns About Present Practices in Pre-First Grade Reading Instruction and Recommendation for Improvement." *Young Children*, Nov. 1986b, vol. 41, pp. 10–13.

National Council of Teachers of English. "Essentials of English." *Language Arts*, Feb. 1983, vol. 60, pp. 244–248.

Schickedanz, J. *Helping Children Learn About Reading.* Washington, D.C.: National Association for the Education of Young Children, 1983.

Schickedanz, J. *More Than the ABCs: The Early Stages of Reading and Writing.* Washington, D.C.: National Association for the Education of Young Children, 1986.

SELECTED
BOOKS
AND
ACTIVITIES

From *Read It Again! Pre–K*, published by GoodYearBooks. Copyright © 1992 Libby Miller and Liz Rothlein.

BROWN BEAR, BROWN BEAR, WHAT DO YOU SEE?

Author
Bill Martin, Jr.

Illustrator
Eric Carle

Publisher
Holt, Rinehart & Winston, Inc., 1967

Pages
26

Other Books by Martin
We know of no other books by the author, however, he has coauthored the following books with John Archambault: *Here Are My Hands, Barn Dance, Ghost-Eye Tree, Knots on a Counting Rope.*

Summary
Brown Bear, Brown Bear, What Do You See? offers a brilliantly illustrated representation of questions and answers about what Brown Bear and other animals see. Colorful animals are shown on bold double-page spreads. A rhyming text allows you to read the questions and the children to provide the answers or vice versa.

Introduction
This is a story about a Brown Bear that sees a redbird. The redbird then sees a yellow duck and on it goes. If you were a bear, what animals do you think you might see?

Discussion Questions

1 What did Brown Bear see? (a redbird looking at him)

2 Which animal in the book did you like best? (answers may vary)

3 Name some of the animals in the story and tell what color they were. (bird, red; duck, yellow; horse, blue; frog, green; cat, purple; dog, white; sheep, black; fish, orange).

4 If Brown Bear lived at the zoo, what other animals might he see? (answers may vary)

5 If the black sheep lived on a farm, what other animals might the sheep see? (answers may vary)

6 Could *Brown Bear, Brown Bear, What Do You See?* be a true story? Why or why not? (Answers may vary but might include "no," because horses aren't blue, cats aren't purple.)

From *Read It Again! Pre–K*, published by GoodYearBooks. Copyright © 1992 Libby Miller and Liz Rothlein.

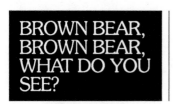

ORAL LANGUAGE ACTIVITY
Directions
Choral-speak and act out the following rhyme:

Brown Bear, Brown Bear, touch the ground.
Brown Bear, Brown Bear, turn around.
Brown Bear, Brown Bear, touch your nose.
Brown Bear, Brown Bear, touch your toes.
Brown Bear, Brown Bear, climb the stairs.
Brown Bear, Brown Bear, say your prayers.
Brown Bear, Brown Bear, shut off the light.
Brown Bear, Brown Bear, say "good night."

Now substitute each of the animal characters for Brown Bear and repeat the rhyme until all the animals have been named (e.g., "Redbird, Redbird, touch the ground. Redbird, Redbird, turn around.") This rhyme may be used with large groups, small groups, or individual children. Assign small groups and individuals a particular animal; they can perform the action mentioned in the rhyme, while the rest of the group chants.

From *Read It Again! Pre-K*, published by GoodYearBooks. Copyright © 1992 Libby Miller and Liz Rothlein.

LEARNING CENTER ACTIVITY
Directions
Place the learning center activity marker at the learning center.
Color the animal pictures on pages 5 and 6 with markers.
Match the color word on the matching word card. Glue the
picture to a piece of cardboard, laminate it, and cut it into puzzle
pieces. Place the puzzle pieces in a coffee can or a box for
storage.

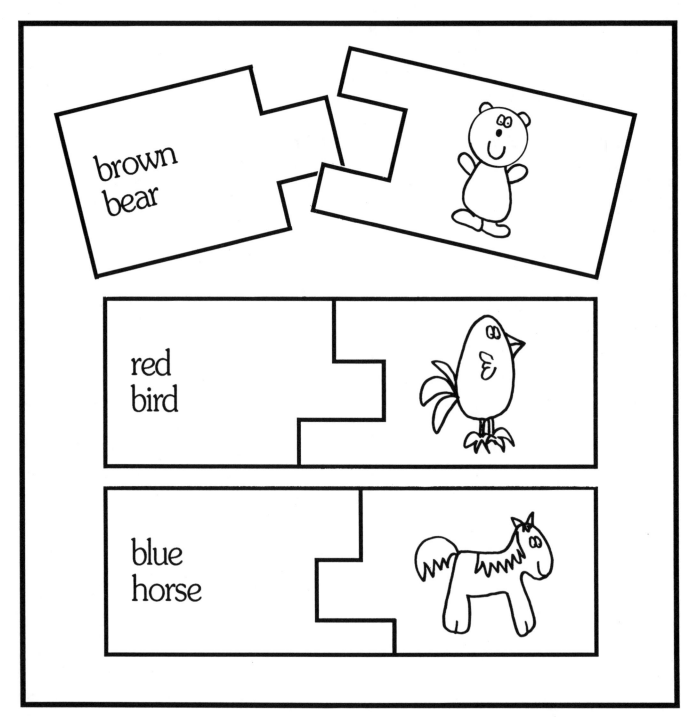

From *Read It Again! Pre-K*, published by GoodYearBooks. Copyright © 1992 Libby Miller and Liz Rothlein.

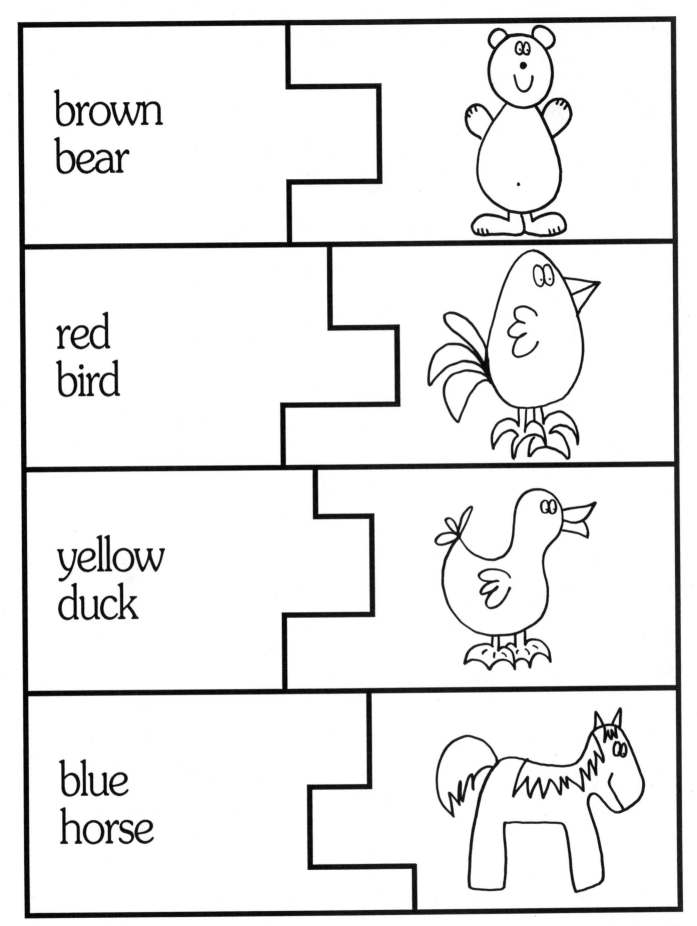

brown
bear

red
bird

yellow
duck

blue
horse

From *Read It Again! Pre-K*, published by GoodYearBooks. Copyright © 1992 Libby Miller and Liz Rothlein.

purple
cat

white
dog

black
sheep

orange
fish

From *Read It Again! Pre-K*, published by GoodYearBooks. Copyright © 1992 Libby Miller and Liz Rothlein.

BROWN BEAR,
BROWN BEAR,
WHAT DO YOU
SEE?

PARENT BULLETIN/HOMEWORK

Name _____ Date _____

We are reading a brilliantly illustrated book *Brown Bear, Brown Bear, What Do You See?* written by Bill Martin, Jr., and illustrated by Eric Carle. This book is about what Brown Bear and other animals *see*. It has a rhyming text and is written in question-and-answer form. If possible, obtain a copy from the library or buy a copy to enjoy with your child. We will be adapting the text to learn about the members of your family.

Follow these directions to help your child make his/her "family" puppets:

Monday: You will need to help your child make one puppet for each member of your family. To make a puppet, fold an 8 1/2" × 11" piece of paper in half (A). (You may choose the size that is most comfortable for your child to use.) Round off the two top corners (B). Glue all around the edges, leaving the bottom edge open so that a hand may be slipped inside (C). Make as many puppets as you have family members.

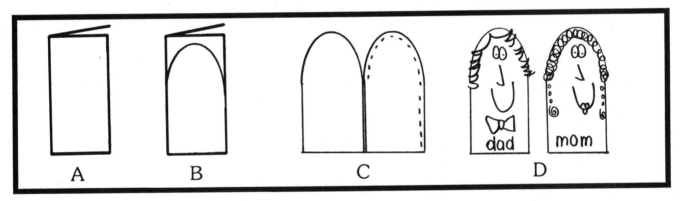

Tuesday: Ask your child to name each member of your family. Talk about first and last names. Discuss the role that each member plays in the family. Ask your child to draw a picture (D) of a family member on each puppet (one person to a puppet). Write the name of the person on the bottom of the puppet.

From *Read It Again! Pre-K*, published by GoodYearBooks. Copyright © 1992 Libby Miller and Liz Rothlein.

Wednesday: Use the adapted rhyme to help your child name everyone in your family. Ask your child to hold up a puppet and use that puppet's name to fill in the spaces. Continue until all of the puppets have been named.

___(Mommy, Mommy,)___ who do you see?

I see ___(Maria)___ looking at me.

___(Maria, Maria,)___ who do you see?

I see _____ looking at me.

Thursday: Add a describing word to the front of the person's name to use in the rhyme.

Example: Pretty Mommy, Pretty Mommy, who do you see? I see Silly Billy looking at me. Silly Billy, Silly Billy, who do you see? I see Happy Harry looking at me. (Words do not have to rhyme.)

Repeat Wednesday's activity using the new words.

Friday: Have your child bring the puppets to school and share them with his/her friends.

Parent's signature: _____

From *Read It Again! Pre-K*, published by GoodYearBooks. Copyright © 1992 Libby Miller and Liz Rothlein.

EVALUATION

Name _____ Date _____

1. Hand the child the *Brown Bear, Brown Bear* book.
   A. Ask the child to show you the front of the book. Is the child able to identify the front of the book? yes _____ no _____
   B. Ask the child to show you the back of the book. Is the child able to identify the back of the book? yes_____ no _____

2. Open to the first page.
   A. Ask the child to point to a letter. Does the child understand the concept of *a letter*? yes _____ no _____
   B. Ask the child to point to a word. Does the child understand the concept of *a word*? yes _____ no_____

3. Ask the child to open the book to the picture of Brown Bear. Have the child "read" from the text. Continue until he/she reaches the blue horse.
   A. Is the child able to "read" (recite) the Brown Bear passage? yes _____ no _____
   B. Is the child able to match the spoken word to the written word by pointing? yes _____ no _____

4. Point to the word *bear*. Is the child able to find another word that looks just like it? yes _____ no _____

From *Read It Again! Pre-K*, published by GoodYearBooks. Copyright © 1992 Libby Miller and Liz Rothlein.

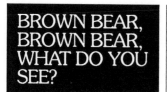

Additional Activities

1 Individual Brown Bear Books

This is an excellent story for the beginning of the year to help children begin to develop listening, speaking, and prereading skills. The activities are *teacher directed* and may be used to integrate a multitude of concepts: colors, shapes, sequencing, animal characteristics, oral language development, direction following, listening skills, cutting, pasting, coloring, and much more.

To make individual big books of *Brown Bear, Brown Bear, What Do You See?* use the direction sheet on page 11. You will need ten, 12" × 18" pieces of paper. Write and copy the text for your big book using the *Brown Bear* book as a guide. Glue the text onto the large sheets of paper to match the illustrations that the children will be making.

It is important to model how to make the animals and to let the children assume much of the responsibility for cutting, coloring, and pasting. When making the bear and the directions call for a circle shape for the head, give the children a square piece of paper that is close to the size of the circle that you want them to make. Have them draw a circle as big as that square, cut it out, and paste it in the appropriate space on their paper. Remember, you are not looking for a "perfectly" finished product but one that is indicative of the child's ability.

2 Asking and Telling

Discuss the difference between an asking sentence (interrogative) and a telling sentence (declarative). Point out that when a sentence demands an answer, it is an asking sentence and a question mark is used. When a sentence tells something, a period is used. To illustrate this concept, read all the asking sentences and have the children respond with the telling sentences. As the story is reread, switch roles and have the children read the asking sentences. Or, divide the children into two groups; one group asks the question and the other group answers.

3 "A Horse of a Different Color" Activity

Cluster animals and their colors in categories such as whether they live in the zoo, farm, or forest, or whether they're pets or silly animals. This cluster is one idea.

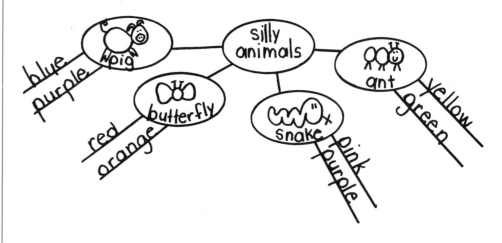

From *Read It Again! Pre-K*, published by GoodYearBooks. Copyright © 1992 Libby Miller and Liz Rothlein.

Brown Bear:
1. Cut circle shapes for head and ears.
2. Add eyes and button nose.
3. Add body (see illustration).

Red Bird:
1. Cut circle shape for body.
2. Add real red feathers.
3. Add beak and feet.

Yellow Duck:
1. Cut large circle shape for body and small circle shape for head.
2. Finger-paint water on paper.
3. Glue duck on water.

Blue Horse:
1. Cut blue oval shape for head.
2. Cut triangle shapes for ears.
3. Cut rectangle shape for neck, with holes punched along the edge for mane.
4. Add blue yarn for mane.
5. Add body.

Green Frog:
1. Cut oval shape for mouth.
2. Add eyes.
3. Add legs using 1" x 6" strips of green paper.
4. Sit frog on green lily pad.

Purple Cat:
1. Cut circle shape for head.
2. Cut triangle shapes for ears.
3. Add toothpicks for whiskers.
4. Add body.

White Dog:
1. Cut rectangle shape for head.
2. Cut triangle shapes for ears.
3. Add a red felt tongue.
4. Draw body.

Black Sheep:
1. Cut oval shape for body.
2. Glue cotton balls on oval.
3. Sprinkle with dry black tempera.

Orange Fish:
1. Cut oval shape for body.
2. Cut triangle shape for fin.
3. Fingerprint scales on fish with orange printer's ink or tempera.

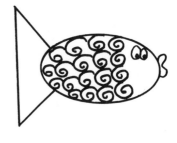

From *Read It Again! Pre-K*, published by GoodYearBooks. Copyright © 1992 Libby Miller and Liz Rothlein.

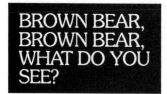

Then use the words to write a new book. For example,

Green Horse, Green Horse,
What do you *see*?

I see a purple snake looking at me.

Continue the story using *Brown Bear, Brown Bear* as a model. Finally, have the children draw a picture of the new animal and place it on the appropriate page in the new book.

Variation: Cluster animals using describing words (adjectives) to tell something about each animal (i.e., slithery snake, hopping kangaroo, skulking lion).

4 Colors, Colors, Colors

Cut out a set of circles for each child. The set should include each of the following colors: brown, red, yellow, blue, green, purple, white, black, and orange. (Since there are several versions of *Brown Bear, Brown Bear*, be sure that the colors used in this activity match the colors mentioned in the book.) Staple the colored circles to straws. Then as you read *Brown Bear, Brown Bear*, ask the children to hold up the color circle for the color being read.

5 Bear Claw Cookies

Using already prepared refrigerator sugar cookie dough or a favorite recipe, make one large dough circle for the bear's paw and five smaller circles for the claws. Attach the five smaller circles to the large circle and bake. Follow the directions on the package or recipe for baking.

6 Phonics: Class "B" Sound Book

Make a beginning sound "b" big book in the shape of a bear. First, draw a 10" circle on a piece of paper. Inside the circle, print the words *I see a _____*. Make a copy for each child. Cut out the circle and attach it to the center of a 12" × 18" piece of construction paper (A).

Discuss what a bear looks like. Then have the children add a circle for the head, half circles for the ears, four legs, and eyes, ears, nose, and mouth (B).

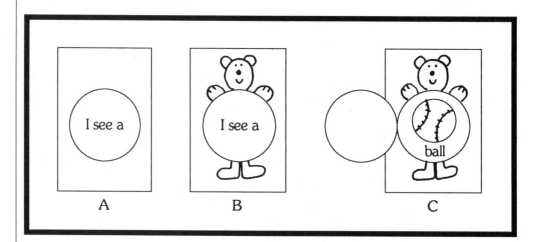

Stop at this point, and ask the children to sit on the floor. Write *I see a _____* on the chalkboard. Talk about Brown Bear. Tell the children that the only things he can see are things that start with the sound at the beginning of the word *bear*. Cluster all the words that begin with the "b" sound on the chalkboard

From *Read It Again! Pre-K*, published by GoodYearBooks. Copyright © 1992 Libby Miller and Liz Rothlein.

or on chart paper. Have the children read the phrase *I see a* _____ and fill in the blank with one of the "b" words. Continue until everyone has had a turn.

Send the children back to their seats to complete their Brown Bear page. Explain that they are to finish their project by drawing a "b" picture under the bear's tummy (circle) (C).

Collect the pages and make them into a class book.

7 Puppets, Puppets, Puppets

Provide materials for the children to make individual puppet sets of the *Brown Bear, Brown Bear* animals. Use the directions and illustrations found on page 11 as a guide. If possible, the children should cut out all shapes. Once the puppets are completed, they may be used in many ways. Role-play the story of *Brown Bear, Brown Bear*, holding up the puppet as the story is being read. Have the children take the puppets home to retell the story to their parents.

Divide the children into two groups. Give each group one set of the puppets. Tell them that the first group to line up in the order that the animals appeared in the story is the winner. Then choral-speak the story as the children hold up their animal puppets.

From *Read It Again! Pre-K*, published by GoodYearBooks. Copyright © 1992 Libby Miller and Liz Rothlein.

THE CARROT SEED

Author
Ruth Krauss

Illustrator
Crockett Johnson

Publisher
Harper & Row, Publishers, Inc.,
1945

Pages
24

Other Books by Krauss
*Is This You?, A Hole Is to Dig,
The Happy Day, Open House
for Butterflies*

Summary
A little boy plants a carrot seed and everyone in his family tells him that it won't come up. The little boy doesn't believe them, so he continues to pull weeds and water the ground. Then, one day, a huge carrot grows, just as the little boy knew it would.

Introduction
Purchase a package of carrot seeds to accompany this introduction. Ask the children if they know where carrots come from. Allow time for them to answer. Then give each child a few seeds to hold in his/her hand. Tell the children that this is a story about a little boy who planted a carrot seed, and although everyone in his family said it wouldn't grow, he believed that it would. He kept pulling the weeds and watering the ground. Ask the children if they have ever tried to grow something from a seed. Allow time for sharing and then read the story.

Discussion Questions

1   Why do you think the little boy planted the carrot seed? (Answers may vary)

2   Why did the little boy's mother, father, and big brother say the seed probably wouldn't come up? (answers may vary)

3   Why did the little boy pull the weeds and sprinkle the ground with water every day? (answers may vary)

4   Do you think the little boy was surprised that his seed grew? (answers may vary)

5   Why do you think it took so long for the carrot seed to grow? (answers may vary)

6   What do you think the little boy will do with his carrot? (answers may vary)

From *Read It Again! Pre–K*, published by GoodYearBooks. Copyright © 1992 Libby Miller and Liz Rothlein.

From *Read It Again! Pre-K*, published by GoodYearBooks. Copyright © 1992 Libby Miller and Liz Rothlein.

THE CARROT SEED

ORAL LANGUAGE ACTIVITY
Directions
Sing to the tune of "Found a Peanut." Make up hand motions to accompany the words in each verse.

Found a carrot seed.
Found a carrot seed.
Found a carrot seed just now.
Just now I found a carrot seed,
Found a carrot seed just now.

Put it in the ground.
Put it in the ground.
Put it in the ground just now.
Just now I put it in the ground,
Put it in the ground just now.

Put some water on it.
Put some water on it.
Put some water on it just now.
Just now I put some water on it,
Put some water on it just now.

The carrot sprouted.
The carrot sprouted.
The carrot sprouted just now.
Just now the carrot sprouted,
The carrot sprouted just now.

The root grew down and fat.
The root grew down and fat.
The root grew down and fat just now.
Just now the root grew down and fat,
The root grew down and fat just now.

Pulled the carrot up.
Pulled the carrot up.
Pulled the carrot up just now.
Just now I pulled the carrot up,
Pulled the carrot up just now.

Washed the dirt off.
Washed the dirt off.
Washed the dirt off just now.
Just now I washed the dirt off,
Washed the dirt off just now.

Took a big bite.
Took a big bite.
Took a big bite just now.
Just now I took a big bite,
Took a big bite just now.

It was yummy.
It was yummy.
It was yummy just now.
Just now it was yummy,
It was yummy just now.

ACTIVITY SHEET
Directions
Make a copy of the activity sheet on page 16 for each child. Discuss each picture and then cut them apart. Use the pictures to accompany the carrot song. When the children sing, have them hold up the picture that matches the verse they are singing. Store the pictures in an envelope.

ORAL LANGUAGE ACTIVITY SHEET

From *Read It Again! Pre–K*, published by GoodYearBooks. Copyright © 1992 Libby Miller and Liz Rothlein.

LEARNING CENTER ACTIVITY
Time to Plant the Carrots: Math Activity
Place the activity marker on page 18 at the learning center.

Materials

Eleven pieces of 6" × 12" green construction paper, 50 carrots from orange construction paper, a felt-tip marker, a stapler, 55 orange carrots, and a large envelope or box to store the completed activity pieces.

Directions

To make the carrot pockets, fold the pieces of construction paper as illustrated below. Write one numeral, 0–10, on the outside of each pocket (see the learning center marker on page 18). Turn the pocket over and draw enough dots to match the numeral on the front. Unfold the pocket, laminate it, refold it, and staple the sides as the dashes indicate.

Using the carrot pattern provided on page 21, trace 55 carrots on a large sheet of orange paper, laminate them, and cut them out.

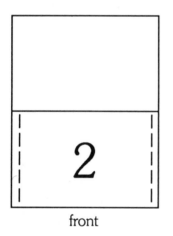

front

back

Finally, lay out the carrots and pockets on a table. Explain to the children that first, they are to put the pockets in a row in numerical order. Then, ask them to place the appropriate number of carrots in each pocket. Once all of the carrots have been "planted," pull the carrots out of the pocket, turn the pocket over and match the number of carrots to the number of dots. Store the pockets and the carrots in a box or large envelope.

From *Read It Again! Pre-K*, published by GoodYearBooks. Copyright © 1992 Libby Miller and Liz Rothlein.

Plant the Carrots

0	 1	2

3	4	5	6

7	8	9	10

From *Read It Again! Pre-K*, published by GoodYearBooks. Copyright © 1992 Libby Miller and Liz Rothlein.

PARENT BULLETIN/HOMEWORK

Name _____ Date _____

We are learning about carrots—how they grow, what they look like, and how they taste. Our interest began when we read *The Carrot Seed* by Ruth Krauss. This is a story about a little boy who planted a carrot seed. Everyone in his family said it wouldn't come up. The little boy didn't believe them. He continued to pull weeds and water the ground around the seed. Then, one day, a huge carrot grew, just as the little boy knew it would.

Please follow the directions below to help your child grow a carrot.

Monday: Collect the following materials for your science experience: a carrot and a shallow dish or pan.

Tuesday: Cut off the top inch of a carrot (see figure A), put it in a shallow pan or dish of water (figure B), and place it on a sunny windowsill. Be sure to add water as it evaporates.

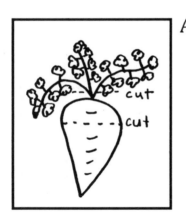

A

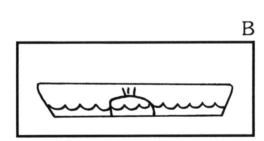

B

Wednesday: Cut out the growth chart on page 20. Reinforce the chart by gluing it to a piece of cardboard. After measuring the plant, chart the growth of the carrot leaves by coloring in the spaces on the chart.

Return Date _____

Have your child bring his/her carrot and growth chart to school on _____ (allow two weeks to complete the experience).

Parent's Signature: _____

From *Read It Again! Pre–K*, published by GoodYearBooks. Copyright © 1992 Libby Miller and Liz Rothlein.

THE CARROT SEED: SCIENCE EXPERIENCE

Name _____ Beginning Date _____

Cut out numbers 8 through 14 (keeping them in a strip); glue them to the top of numbers 1 through 7 to make a chart that measures to 14 inches.

Glue #8 here		
7		14
6		13
5		12
4		11
3		10
2		9
1		8

From *Read It Again! Pre-K*, published by GoodYearBooks. Copyright © 1992 Libby Miller and Liz Rothlein.

EVALUATION

Name _____ Date _____

1. Is the child able to name the three things that the little boy did with his seed in the story?

    _____ He planted the seed.
    _____ He watered the seed.
    _____ He pulled the weeds.

2. Is the child able to tell what happened to the seed? (it grew into a carrot)
    yes _____ no _____

3. Can the child name two things that can be done with a carrot besides growing? Write the child's answers in the space provided.

    A. _____

    B. _____

4. Can the child name the part of the plant that we eat when we eat a carrot? (root)
    yes _____ no _____

Carrot Pattern

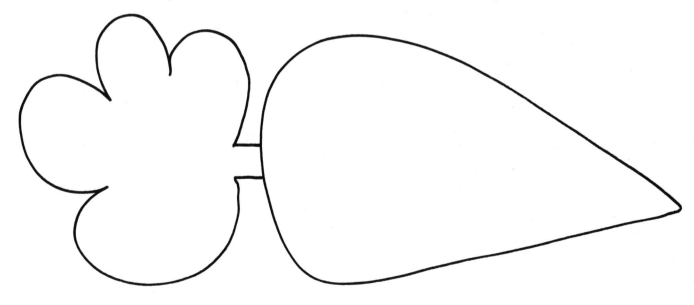

From *Read It Again! Pre–K*, published by GoodYearBooks. Copyright © 1992 Libby Miller and Liz Rothlein.

Additional Activities

1 Carrot and Raisin Salad

Make a copy of the recipe cards on pages 24 and 25 and laminate them.
Arrange the cards in the order shown in the recipe card below, along with the
ingredients and utensils, in the cooking center.

Carrot and Raisin Salad

1 carrot per child
wax paper
grater
2 small bowls
1 5-oz. paper cup per child
raisins
tablespoons
mayonnaise or salad dressing
1 plastic spoon per child

Wash hands.
Grate carrots over wax paper.
Put grated carrots in paper cup.
Add 5 raisins.
Add 1 tablespoon mayonnaise or salad dressing.
Stir.

Model how to follow the steps for making the salad. Then step back, watch
the activity, and enjoy!

2 How Many Ways Can You Eat a Carrot?

Discuss the ways in which a carrot can be eaten: raw, cooked, juiced, or baked in
cakes, cookies, and muffins. Following this discussion, plan a carrot-tasting party;
ask parents to provide a variety of carrot dishes.

3 Carrots Are Vegetables

Tell the children that carrots are vegetables. Discuss what a vegetable is and then
have the children name some vegetables. Make a list of the vegetables on the
chalkboard: peas, beans, squash, cauliflower, Brussels sprouts, broccoli, corn,
spinach, lettuce. Pass out a variety of seed catalogs and magazines. Ask the
children to look through the magazines and cut out all the vegetables that they
can find. Finally, provide large sheets of paper to make a vegetable collage of all
their pictures.

4 Sprout a Carrot

Materials for Each Child: A few carrot seeds, a wet paper towel, and ziplock
plastic bag.

Sprinkle the seeds on the wet paper towel, and close the bag. Tape each
child's name on the bag, and place the bags on a sunny windowsill. Check the
bags daily to see if the seeds have sprouted. Once they have sprouted, they can
be planted in small Styrofoam cups (which have had holes punched in the bottom
for drainage) and filled with soil. After planting the seeds, the children can
observe their plants and discuss what they see happening.

From *Read It Again! Pre–K*, published by GoodYearBooks. Copyright © 1992 Libby Miller and Liz Rothlein.

Welcome to Westfield Washington Public Library - Westfield! You checked out the following items:

1. Read It Again! pre-K: introducing literature to young children
Barcode: 78292000117698
Due: 2012-03-17 11:59 PM
Renewal(s) Remaining: 1

2. Story stretchers: activities to expand children's favorite books
Barcode: 78292000060421
Due: 2012-03-17 11:59 PM
Renewal(s) Remaining: 1

WWPL W 2012-02-25 13:24
You were helped by staff of the Westfield Washington Public Library

5 **Carrot-Seed Journals**

As a follow-up activity to the planting experience, have each child make "My Carrot-Seed Journal" in which he/she records what happens from the time the carrot seeds are planted to when they grow. For example, on page 1, the children can draw a picture of planting the seed; on page 2, a picture of watering it. If individual journals are not feasible, make a "Class Carrot-Seed Journal."

> ## My Carrot-Seed Journal

6 **Carrot Prints**

Materials:
- carrots cut in half
- orange tempera paint
- a large sheet of paper
- paper plate

Spread orange tempera paint on a paper plate. Have the children dip the carrots in the paint and then print on the sheets of paper. Emphasize the color *orange* by writing the word on the chalkboard and placing a sheet with orange carrot prints next to it. Discuss and list other things that are orange.

7 **Carrot, Carrot, Who Has the Carrot?**

Seat the children in a circle. Play some music as a carrot is passed from child to child. When the music stops, the child holding the carrot is asked to name another vegetable. Encourage the children to think of vegetables that have not been named before. *Note:* This is a good follow-up to activity number 3: making a vegetable collage.

8 **Which Carrot Stick Is the Longest?**

Materials: Carrot sticks of different lengths (3 to a ziplock plastic bag) and a paper towel for each child.

Have the children wash their hands. Then ask them to arrange their carrot strips from longest to shortest on the paper towel. Have the children take a bite off the end of one carrot stick. Ask them questions such as, what happens when they take a bite? Does the carrot get longer or shorter? Are the carrots still in the right order from the longest to the shortest?

From *Read It Again! Pre-K*, published by GoodYearBooks. Copyright © 1992 Libby Miller and Liz Rothlein.

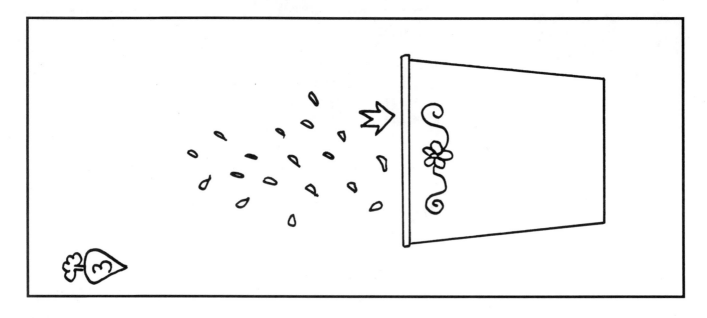

From *Read It Again! Pre–K*, published by GoodYearBooks. Copyright © 1992 Libby Miller and Liz Rothlein.

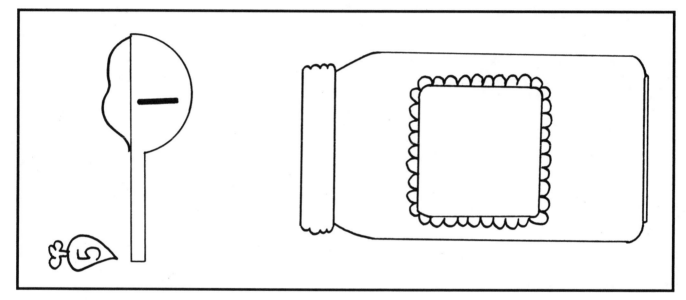

From *Read It Again! Pre-K*, published by GoodYearBooks. Copyright © 1992 Libby Miller and Liz Rothlein.

DO YOU WANT TO BE MY FRIEND?

Author/Illustrator
Eric Carle

Publisher
Thomas Y. Crowell Co.

Pages
28

Other Books by Carle
*The Very Hungry Caterpillar,
The Mixed-Up Chameleon, The
Secret Birthday Message,
Grouchy Ladybug, Have You
Seen My Cat?, House for
Hermit Crab, 1,2,2, to the Zoo,
Rooster's Off to See the World,
Tiny Seed, The Very Busy
Spider*

Summary
In this story, a mouse goes around asking the tails of other animals if they want to be his friend. After asking a series of animal's tails if they want to be his friend, he asks the right tail and finds a friend.

Introduction
This is a story about a little mouse who asked many animals if they wanted to be his friend. Have you ever wanted someone to be your friend? Explain.

Discussion Questions

1 Who was the mouse looking for? (a friend)

2 Name some of the animals that the little mouse asked to be his friend. (answers may vary)

3 Do you think it was a good idea that he asked the animals that he did ask to be his friend? (answers may vary)

4 What do you think some of the animals thought when this little mouse asked them to be his friend? (answers may vary)

5 Did the mouse find what he was looking for? Explain. (Yes, because he found a friend.)

6 What do you think the mouse did after he found a friend? (answers may vary)

From *Read It Again! Pre–K*, published by GoodYearBooks. Copyright © 1992 Libby Miller and Liz Rothlein.

ORAL LANGUAGE ACTIVITY
Directions

After rereading *Do You Want to Be My Friend?* make a cluster of all the animals seen in the story. Have the children draw one of the animals found in the cluster on a 6" × 6" piece of paper. Label the animals and staple them to headbands for the children to wear while singing the following song. Sing the song to the tune of *"The Farmer in the Dell."*

The mouse wants a friend.
The mouse wants a friend.
Hi, Ho, the merry-o,
The mouse wants a friend.

The mouse finds a horse.
The mouse finds a horse.
Hi, Ho, the merry-o,
The mouse finds a horse.

Continue adding verses to the song in the same manner as the first two verses: the mouse finds a bird, the mouse finds an alligator, the mouse finds a lion, the mouse finds a hippopotamus, the mouse finds a seal, the mouse finds a monkey, the mouse finds a peacock, the mouse finds a fox, the mouse finds a kangaroo, the mouse finds a giraffe, the mouse finds a snake. End the song with the following verse:

The mouse finds a friend.
The mouse finds a friend.
Hi, Ho, the merry-o,
The mouse finds a friend.

From *Read It Again! Pre-K*, published by GoodYearBooks. Copyright © 1992 Libby Miller and Liz Rothlein.

LEARNING CENTER ACTIVITY
Animal Lotto

Directions

Place the learning center activity marker (p. 31) at the center.

Cut out the pictures on pages 29 and 30, glue them to cardboard, laminate, and cut the pictures apart into puzzle pieces.

This activity is played like the game Concentration.

1. Place the animal puzzle pieces facedown on the table or play area.
2. The first child chooses two pieces to turn over. If the animal body and tail match, the child may keep the pieces and take another turn. If the pieces do not match, the child turns both pieces over and the next child takes a turn.
3. Continue in this manner until all the animals have been matched.

Demonstrate this activity for the children, and provide time for them to visit the center.

From *Read It Again! Pre-K*, published by GoodYearBooks. Copyright © 1992 Libby Miller and Liz Rothlein.

From *Read It Again! Pre-K*, published by GoodYearBooks. Copyright © 1992 Libby Miller and Liz Rothlein.

From *Read It Again! Pre–K*, published by GoodYearBooks. Copyright © 1992 Libby Miller and Liz Rothlein.

Find My Tail!

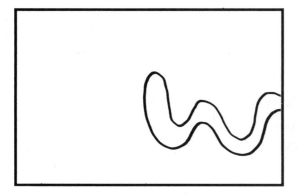 

From *Read It Again! Pre–K*, published by GoodYearBooks. Copyright © 1992 Libby Miller and Liz Rothlein.

PARENT BULLETIN/HOMEWORK

Name _____ Date _____

We are reading *Do You Want to Be My Friend?* by Eric Carle. This book is about a little mouse that asks the tails of many different animals if they will be his friend. The animal's tail is shown on one page, and the next page shows the animal that goes with the tail. The animals that the mouse asks to be his friend include a horse, bird, alligator, lion, hippopotamus, seal, monkey, peacock, fox, kangaroo, giraffe, snake, and finally another mouse.

   The following game will be fun for you and your child to play as you reinforce beginning sounds. Glue pages 32 and 33 to a piece of cardboard (a cereal box would work). Cut the pieces apart, mix them up, and then help your child match the correct beginning letter to the animal that begins with that sound.

mouse

peacock

From *Read It Again! Pre–K*, published by GoodYearBooks. Copyright © 1992 Libby Miller and Liz Rothlein.

snake

giraffe

lion

horse

From *Read It Again! Pre-K*, published by GoodYearBooks. Copyright © 1992 Libby Miller and Liz Rothlein.

EVALUATION

Name _____ Date _____

1. Is the child able to retell the story with a beginning, middle, and end?   yes   no
2. Is the child able to tell who the mouse is looking for? (a friend)   yes   no
3. What does the child think the mouse did after finding his friend?   yes   no

Now have the child look at the words in the box below. Then answer the following questions.

Do you want to be my friend?

---

4. Is the child able to "read" or recite the words to the sentence in the box?   yes   no
5. Is the child able to match the spoken word to the printed word when you point to it?   yes   no
6. Is the child able to point to the first word in the sentence?   yes   no
7. Is the child able to point to the word *my*?   yes   no

From *Read It Again! Pre–K*, published by GoodYearBooks. Copyright © 1992 Libby Miller and Liz Rothlein.

Additional Activities

1 Phonics: Class "M" Sound Book

Make an initial-sound class book for the letter *m* sound. Brainstorm and cluster words that begin with *m*. Write the words on a large sheet of paper or on the chalkboard so they may be used as a reference when you make the pages of the book.

Additional "m" words: mop, monkey, measuring cup, motorboat, mitten, mug, moon, money, marble, mirror, mud.

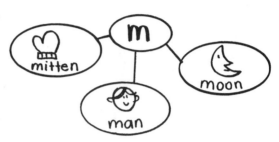

Provide each child with a preprinted page, as shown on page 37. Ask them to choose a word from the cluster, write it in the blank, and illustrate that word on the page provided. Encourage the children to use their crayons to draw the picture and to make their illustration as large as the space within the circle.

This page will then become a page in the class book. Try to use as many different words as possible. Make the cover for the class book by cutting a circle out of construction paper the size of the worksheet on page 37. Next cut two circles from construction paper for the ears. Add them to the circle. Add eyes (use wiggle eyes, adhesive dots, construction paper or felt markers or crayons) and a construction-paper nose. Punch holes near the nose and thread yarn through for whiskers.

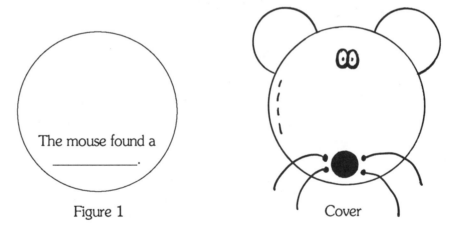

The mouse found a
_____.

Figure 1   Cover

2 Fingerprint Mice

Give each child a piece of 6" × 6" paper, ink pads, and fine-point markers. Demonstrate how to make mouse prints with fingers using the ink pad and paper. Using the fine-point markers, add ears, whiskers, eyes, a tail, and legs.

From *Read It Again! Pre-K*, published by GoodYearBooks. Copyright © 1992 Libby Miller and Liz Rothlein.

3 Where Can You Find Me? – Classification Activity

Have the children recall all the animals found in the book and list them on the chalkboard. (bird, alligator, lion, hippopotamus, seal, monkey, peacock, fox, kangaroo, giraffe, snake, and a mouse) Classify the animals into the following groups.

Zoo Animals   Farm Animals   Circus Animals   Other Animals

After they have classified these animals, ask them to name other animals that would fit into these categories and list them on the board.

4 Snake Bulletin Board

Create a bulletin board by making a long snake out of green construction paper (see the illustration of the snake in the book) that will stretch along the bulletin board or chalkboard. Next, provide a variety of materials: construction paper, yarn, fur, fabrics, feathers. Ask each child to create one of the animals that the mouse asked to be his friend. Then make an animal mural by putting each animal on the snake.

5 Asking and Telling

The focus of this activity is to introduce the concept of asking sentences and telling sentences. Have the children pretend that they are going on a trip to look for a friend. Decide, as a group, where they would go (i.e., farm, circus, zoo, grocery store, museum, moon). Write their chosen destination on the chalkboard. With the children, cluster all the kinds of animals and people they might see at this place.

Have the children choose an animal or person from the cluster that they would like to draw on a 6" × 6" piece of manila paper. Staple the completed picture on a piece of sentence

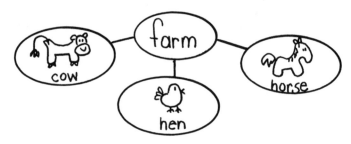

strip (big enough to fit around the child's head). Let the children wear their friends as a headband.

Use the headbands to act out the following question and answer activity sung to the tune of "Mary Had a Little Lamb."

Question: Do you want to be my friend,
be my friend, be my friend?
Do you want to be my friend?
The <u>mousie</u> asked the <u>horse</u>.

Answer: Yes I want to be your friend,
be your friend, be your friend?
Yes I want to be your friend.
Please come and play with me.

Substitute other animals or personalities for the animals that are underlined.

From *Read It Again! Pre-K*, published by GoodYearBooks. Copyright © 1992 Libby Miller and Liz Rothlein.

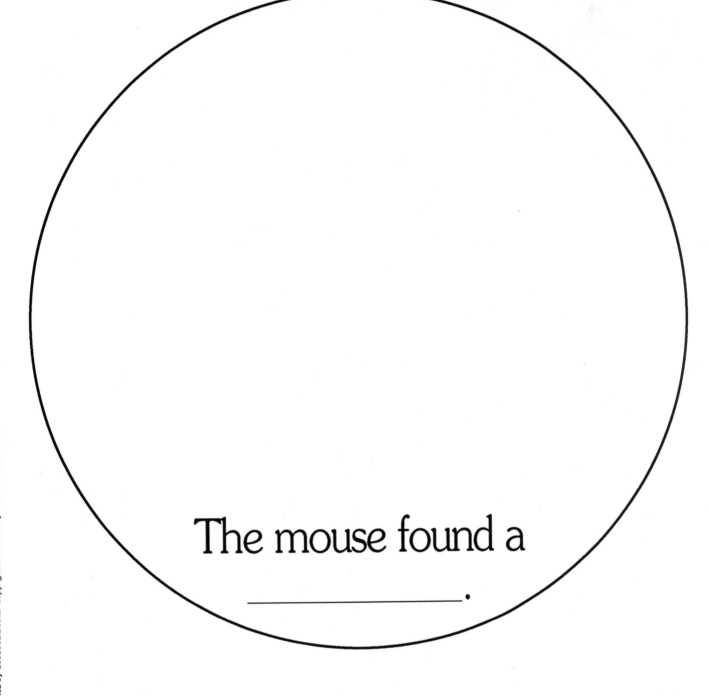

The mouse found a
_____.

From *Read It Again! Pre-K*, published by GoodYearBooks. Copyright © 1992 Libby Miller and Liz Rothlein.

GOODNIGHT MOON

Author
Margaret Wise Brown

Illustrator
Clement Hurd

Publisher
Harper & Row, Publishers, Inc.,
1947

Pages
30

Other Books by Brown
*The Important Book, Little Fur
Family, Margaret Wise Brown's
Wonderful Storybook, The
Runaway Bunny, The Sailor
Dog, When the Wind Blew*

Summary
Goodnight Moon is about a little rabbit that says goodnight to all the familiar things in his room as well as to the moon. It is written in rhyme.

Introduction
Goodnight Moon is a story about a little rabbit that says goodnight to the many different things he can see from his bed. For example, he says goodnight to the kittens, the mittens, the house, the mouse, and even the moon. He finally falls asleep, and his room is dark and quiet. Who or what do you say goodnight to before you go to sleep?

Discussion Questions

1 What were some of the animals that the little rabbit said goodnight to? (answers may vary but may include cow jumping over the moon, three little bears, two kittens, a mouse)

2 Why do you think the little rabbit said goodnight to so many things before he could go to sleep? (answers many vary)

3 The little rabbit said goodnight to many things. What are some things you do before you go to sleep at night? (answers may vary)

4 How do you think the rabbit felt about going to sleep? (answers may vary)

5 Why do you think the mittens and socks were hanging on the clothesline? (answers may vary but may include that they needed to dry)

6 Who do you think the grown-up rabbit in the chair was? (answers may vary but may include mother or grandmother) Why do you think she was there? (answers may vary)

From *Read It Again! Pre–K*, published by GoodYearBooks. Copyright © 1992 Libby Miller and Liz Rothlein.

ORAL LANGUAGE ACTIVITY
Directions

Using the rhyming words from the story, choral-speak the following. Allow the children to chant a rhyming word for each line. Hold up the picture cards from the learning center activity on pages 40 and 41 as the rhyming words are spoken.

Goodnight, goodnight, goodnight, kittens.
Goodnight, goodnight, goodnight, _____. (mittens)

Goodnight, goodnight, goodnight, mouse.
Goodnight, goodnight, goodnight, _____. (house)

Goodnight, goodnight, goodnight, mush.
Goodnight, goodnight, goodnight, _____. (brush)

Goodnight, goodnight, goodnight, clocks.
Goodnight, goodnight, goodnight, _____. (socks)

After completing this chant, make up your own rhyming word chant using rhyming words that are not found in the story. Have children illustrate each new word on a 6" × 6" piece of tagboard and label it. New pictures may be held up when saying the new chant.

Goodnight, goodnight, goodnight, man.
Goodnight, goodnight, goodnight, _____. (pan, fan)

Goodnight, goodnight, goodnight, bed.
Goodnight, goodnight, goodnight, _____. (Ted, red)

Goodnight, goodnight, goodnight, pig.
Goodnight, goodnight, goodnight, _____. (wig, fig)

Goodnight, goodnight, goodnight, car.
Goodnight, goodnight, goodnight, _____. (star, jar)

From *Read It Again! Pre-K*, published by GoodYearBooks. Copyright © 1992 Libby Miller and Liz Rothlein.

LEARNING CENTER ACTIVITY
Time to Rhyme Center: Concentration

Directions
Place **Time to Rhyme Center** activity marker (page 42) at the learning center.

Cut out the pictures (on pages 40 & 41) and glue them to index cards to make playing cards. Play concentration using the cards by following these directions:

1. Turn cards facedown.
2. Player 1 turns over two cards. If the cards match, the player may keep the cards. If the cards do not match, they are placed facedown on the playing space.
3. Then, player 2 turns over two cards and follows the same procedures as player 1.
4. Continue until all matches have been made.

From *Read It Again! Pre-K*, published by GoodYearBooks. Copyright © 1992 Libby Miller and Liz Rothlein.

From *Read It Again! Pre-K*, published by GoodYearBooks. Copyright © 1992 Libby Miller and Liz Rothlein.

Time to Rhyme Center

Concentration

From *Read It Again! Pre–K*, published by GoodYearBooks. Copyright © 1992 Libby Miller and Liz Rothlein.

From *Read It Again! Pre-K*, published by GoodYearBooks. Copyright © 1992 Libby Miller and Liz Rothlein.

GOODNIGHT MOON

PARENT BULLETIN/HOMEWORK

Name _____ Date _____

This week we are reading *Goodnight Moon* by Margaret Wise Brown. It is a story about a little rabbit who says goodnight to the many different things he can see from his bed before he falls asleep. He says goodnight to mittens, kittens, a brush, the mush, bears, chairs, spoons, and even the moon.

   In this book, illustrations show a full moon as it crosses the sky. Using the calendar below, chart how the moon looks each night. To do this, go outside with your child and look into the night sky, and then have your child draw how the moon looks on the *Goodnight Moon* calendar. This activity will help your child see how the moon gradually changes over a period of a month. You may want to get a copy of *Moon Seems to Change* by F. Branley. This book explains why the moon appears to change shapes at different times.

Goodnight Moon

SUNDAY	MONDAY	TUESDAY	WEDNESDAY	THURSDAY	FRIDAY	SATURDAY

1. Is the child able to "hear" rhyming words? Say the following pairs of words and have the child respond by raising a hand when the pairs rhyme. Circle yes if the child responds correctly or no if the child responds incorrectly. Give the following example before beginning the evaluation:

Practice

cat – hat   Tell the child to raise his/her hand because the two words rhyme.

apple – alligator   Tell the child to lower his/her hand because the two words do not rhyme.

A. mouse – house   yes   no   F. man – map   yes   no
B. car – cat   yes   no   G. plane – train yes   no
C. pig – jig   yes   no   H. soap – sock   yes   no
D. hair – bear   yes   no   I. sky – pie   yes   no
E. blue – boy   yes   no   J. red – bed   yes   no

2. This activity evaluates the child's concepts of print.
   Directions (for worksheet on page 45).
   Have the child cut apart the words on the solid lines at the top of the page and then paste them in order in the long narrow box under his/her name. Then ask the child to illustrate the sentence in the large box using crayons.

   A. Did the child paste the words in order from left to right? yes ____ no ____
   B. Are all of the words "right-side-up"? yes ____ no ____
   C. Does the child's picture relate to the sentence? yes ____ no ____

   Ask the child to read the words and point to each word as he/she reads it.

   D. Is the child able to "read" the sentence? yes ____ no ____
      (Remember, reading at this level means has the child memorized the sentence.)
   E. Does the child match the spoken word to the written word while reading and pointing? yes ____ no ____

From *Read It Again! Pre–K*, published by GoodYearBooks. Copyright © 1992 Libby Miller and Liz Rothlein.

moon	Goodnight

Name _____ Date _____

From *Read It Again! Pre-K*, published by GoodYearBooks. Copyright © 1992 Libby Miller and Liz Rothlein.

Additional Activities

1 Phonics: Class "G" Sound Book

Make a Goodnight g _____ book. Have the children cluster all the words that they can think of that begin with the hard "g" sound (i.e., goat, girl). Write the words on a large sheet of paper or on the chalkboard so that they can be used for reference when making the pages of the book.

Give each child a copy of the worksheet on page 48. Model how to draw a picture in the box provided on the worksheet. Encourage the children to use their crayons to draw the picture and to make the picture as big as the space. Demonstrate how to color the picture using controlled strokes. Model how to write the "g" word on the line below the picture using a pencil. Put the completed pages into a class book for everyone to enjoy.

2

Make rhyming headbands by cutting out the rhyming pictures on pages 40 and 41. Staple each picture to a length of sentence strip or to a piece of paper that is long enough to fit around the child's head. Use the headbands for acting out the story *Goodnight Moon*. Read the story. As the rhyming words are read, have the children listen for the word represented on their headbands and come forward when they hear it. They could also put on the headbands and look for someone with a rhyming headband.

3

Read other books about moons: *Many Moons* by James Thurber, *Moon Tiger* by P. Root, *Mooncake* or *Moongame* by F. Asch, *Moonlight* by J. Ormond. Compare and contrast these books with *Goodnight Moon*.

4

Using the recipe below, make Cheese Moons for snacktime:

Cheese Moons

2 cups grated cheddar cheese
2 cups whole wheat flour
1/2 cup vegetable oil
Add water to moisten

Stir all the ingredients together. Refrigerate the mixture for about 30 minutes. Give each child a tablespoon of dough. Tell them to roll the dough into a small ball (the moon). Place the cheese moons on a greased cookie sheet, and bake them 12–15 minutes in a 400° oven. This recipe makes approximately 40 cheese moons.

---

5 Pop-Up Rhyming Book

Materials needed for each book: a copy of the pop-up book worksheet on pages 49 and 50, scissors, crayons and/or markers, 1 piece of 4" × 4" construction paper, glue

Before making the pop-up book, discuss the rhyming words in *Goodnight Moon* (i.e., bears–chairs, kittens–mittens, mush–brush, clocks–socks). Cluster the rhyming pairs on the chalkboard.

From *Read It Again! Pre–K*, published by GoodYearBooks. Copyright © 1992 Libby Miller and Liz Rothlein.

From *Read It Again! Pre-K*, published by GoodYearBooks. Copyright © 1992 Libby Miller and Liz Rothlein.

GOODNIGHT MOON

Other rhyming words may be added to the cluster.

Directions

You will need to prepare the worksheet for the pop-up book by following steps A–C for Pre-K children and some kindergarten children.

A. Fold the pop-up worksheet (side 1) on the solid line.

B. Cut on dotted lines *a* and *b*.

C. Push solid line *c* to the inside of the folded paper so that lines *d* and *e* touch.

D. Have the children choose a pair of rhyming words for their rhyming pop-up book. They should use crayons or markers to draw *one* of the rhyming words on the front of the now-folded piece of paper. Write the name of the rhyming word on the line next to *Goodnight*.

E. On a 4" × 4" piece of paper, have the children draw a picture of a word that rhymes with the picture on side 1. Write the name of the rhyming word on the line (on side 2) next to *Goodnight*.

F. Glue the completed picture to the front of the pop-up tab on the inside of side 2. When the book is opened, the picture on the inside will pop up.

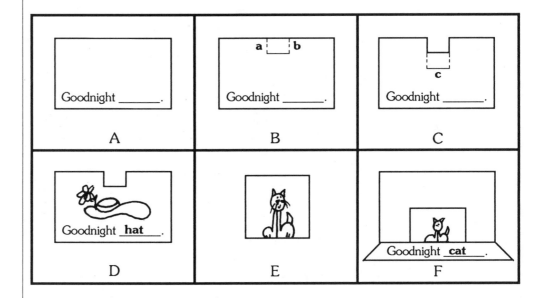

Goodnight g _____

From *Read It Again! Pre–K*, published by GoodYearBooks. Copyright © 1992 Libby Miller and Liz Rothlein.

d

a

b

c

e

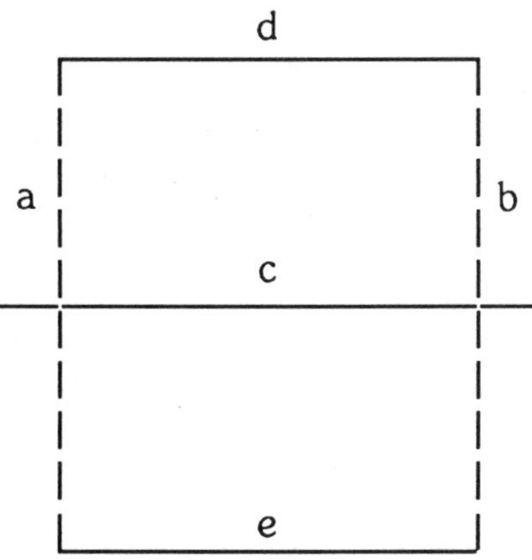

Goodnight _____

From *Read It Again! Pre-K*, published by GoodYearBooks. Copyright © 1992 Libby Miller and Liz Rothlein.

Goodnight _____

SIDE 2

From *Read It Again! Pre–K*, published by GoodYearBooks. Copyright © 1992 Libby Miller and Liz Rothlein.

HERE ARE MY HANDS

Authors
Bill Martin, Jr., and
John Archambault

Illustrator
Ted Rand

Publisher
Henry Holt & Co., Inc., 1987

Pages
25

Other Books by Martin and Archambault
Barn Dance, Ghost-Eye Tree, Knots On a Counting Rope, Listen to the Rain, White Dynamite and Curly Kidd.
NOTE: Bill Martin, Jr., is the author of *Brown Bear, Brown Bear, What Do You See?*

Summary
Here Are My Hands uses simple phrases and rhymes to identify key parts of the human body and their functions. Children representing a variety of ethnic backgrounds are featured throughout the book.

Introduction
This story tells about the different parts of our body and what they do. Can you tell me the names of some of your body parts and what they do?

Discussion Questions

1   Name the body parts that were mentioned in the story and tell what they do. (answers may vary)

2   This story says that hands are for catching and throwing. What are some other things that you can use your hands for? (answers may vary)

3   What are some body parts that were not mentioned in the story? (answers may vary)

4   This story said, "Here is my elbow, my arm, and my chin," but it did not say what these body parts do. What is your chin used for? What do you use your arms for? What does your elbow do, and what is it used for? (answers may vary)

5   In this story, many words rhyme: *chin* and *in, crying* and *drying, knowing* and *blowing.* What are some other rhyming words? (answers may vary)

6   The title of this book is *Here Are My Hands.* Do you think this is a good title? Why or why not? (answers may vary)

From *Read It Again! Pre-K,* published by GoodYearBooks. Copyright © 1992 Libby Miller and Liz Rothlein.

ORAL LANGUAGE ACTIVITY
Directions

Using the tune of "Did You Ever See a Lassie?" sing and dramatize "Have You Ever Seen My Hands?" Additional verses may be added to emphasize different body parts: Have you ever seen my feet jump up and down? Have you ever seen my eyes open and close?

Have you ever seen my hands,
My hands, my hands,
Have you ever seen my hands,
Clap fast and loud?

Clap fast and loud,
Clap fast and loud,
Have you ever seen my hands,
Clap fast and loud?

Have you ever seen my hands,
My hands, my hands,
Have you ever seen my hands,
Clap soft and slow?

Clap soft and slow,
Clap soft and slow,
Have you ever seen my hands,
Clap soft and slow?

Have you ever seen my hands,
My hands, my hands,
Have you ever seen my hands,
Wiggle up and down?

Wiggle up and down,
Wiggle up and down,
Have you ever seen my hands,
Wiggle up and down?

Have you ever seen my hands,
My hands, my hands,
Have you ever seen my hands,
Shake in front and in back?

Shake in front and in back,
Shake in front and in back,
Have you ever seen my hands,
Shake in front and in back?

From *Read It Again! Pre–K*, published by GoodYearBooks. Copyright © 1992 Libby Miller and Liz Rothlein.

LEARNING CENTER ACTIVITY
Mr. Five Senses

Here Are My Hands is an excellent way to introduce the five senses. These activities are devised to help children learn how their eyes, ears, hands, nose, and mouth help them tell about the world around them. The projects are designed for learning centers or for small group instruction and participation.

Place the science center activity marker (p. 55) at the learning station.

Sense of Sight

Materials: Sense of Sight Activity sheet (p. 56); these objects: crayon, flower, button, paintbrush, pencil, paper clip, book, scissors, eraser, block, ball, puzzle piece, yarn, apple, mug; and a tray.

Provide children with a copy of the activity sheet. Then place 10 of the 15 objects listed in the materials section on a tray. Have each child look carefully at the tray for 15 to 20 seconds. Then take the tray away. Tell the children to circle all the pictures of the objects that they saw on the tray and put an X on the objects that they did not see. Check the answers with the children by holding up each object and matching it to the answer sheet.

Sense of Taste

Materials: Wax paper, 3 spoons, salt, sugar, and flour.

Tear off a piece of wax paper for each child. Place a small amount of each substance—salt, sugar, and flour—on the wax paper. Ask the children what sense they will use to identify the substances. Since all of the powders look the same, they will have to use their sense of "taste." Allow the children to taste and identify the substances.

From *Read It Again! Pre-K*, published by GoodYearBooks. Copyright © 1992 Libby Miller and Liz Rothlein.

Sense of Smell

Materials: 5 cotton balls, coffee crystals, cinnamon, garlic, onion, vinegar, 5 small paper cups, tinfoil.

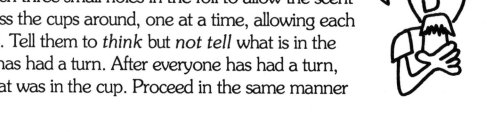

Sprinkle one cotton ball with coffee, one with cinnamon, and so forth. Place the cotton balls in the cups and cover them tightly with a piece of tinfoil. Punch three small holes in the foil to allow the scent to escape. Next, pass the cups around, one at a time, allowing each child a turn to smell. Tell them to *think* but *not tell* what is in the cup until everyone has had a turn. After everyone has had a turn, ask the children what was in the cup. Proceed in the same manner with the next cup.

Sense of Hearing

Materials: Instruments such as rhythm sticks, sand blocks, finger cymbals, triangles, bells, and maracas, and 5 blindfolds.

Show the children all the instruments and demonstrate each of their sounds. Blindfold five children. Make sounds using each instrument. Have the children hold up their hands if they can identify the sound. Continue the activity using a variety of instruments.

Sense of Touch

Materials: glue, felt-tip marker, 2 sets of 5 objects (2 buttons, 2 pieces of sandpaper, 1 marble) 5 paper or cloth bags, and a 3" × 10" piece of cardboard.

Glue one of each of the five objects on the cardboard and label it. Place the matching object in a bag. Allow time for children to feel the object in the bag and then guess what they think the object is. They can check their answers by matching the object to the object board.

From *Read It Again! Pre-K*, published by GoodYearBooks. Copyright © 1992 Libby Miller and Liz Rothlein.

From *Read It Again! Pre-K*, published by GoodYearBooks. Copyright © 1992 Libby Miller and Liz Rothlein.

SENSE OF SIGHT ACTIVITY SHEET

Name _____ Date _____

red

From *Read It Again! Pre–K*, published by GoodYearBooks. Copyright © 1992 Libby Miller and Liz Rothlein.

From *Read It Again! Pre-K*, published by GoodYearBooks. Copyright © 1992 Libby Miller and Liz Rothlein.

HERE ARE MY HANDS

Name _____ Date _____

The homework for this week reinforces the book that we are reading in class. In a rhythmic, predictable manner, *Here Are My Hands*, by Bill Martin, Jr., and John Archambault, tells about different body parts and what they do. Please follow the directions to help your child learn the name and location of some very important parts of the human body.

Monday: Have your child name the different parts of his/her body as you write them down on a large sheet of paper. This technique is called *clustering*, and it is an activity we do at school to help children focus on a specific concept. In addition to the body parts your child names, point out and write down body parts your child did not mention.

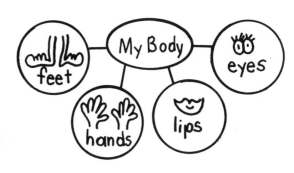

Tuesday and Wednesday: Do one of the following activities:
1. Have your child draw his/her body on a very large sheet of paper. Encourage your child to draw the body "as big as the paper" using crayons and/or markers.
2. Find a sheet of paper large enough for your child to lie down on. Trace around his/her body. Have your child fill in the features with marker, crayon, or paints.

Thursday: Have your child cut out the labels below. Help him/her match the labels to the body parts you drew on Tuesday and Wednesday. Paste or glue labels onto the body. Read sentences with your child by pointing to the words as you read. (Thursday's activity is appropriate for mature kindergarten and first-grade students.)

Friday: Have your child bring his/her completed body to school.

Here is my hand.	Here is my mouth.
Here is my eye.	Here is my tongue.
Here is my neck.	Here is my foot.
Here is my nose.	Here is my knee.
Here is my elbow.	Here is my ear.

1. This section evaluates the child's awareness of his/her body.
    A. Is the child able to name the following parts of the body when you point to them?

eyes	yes _____	no _____	nose	yes _____	no _____
ears	yes _____	no _____	elbows	yes _____	no _____
neck	yes _____	no _____	cheeks	yes _____	no _____
heel	yes _____	no _____	wrist	yes _____	no _____
chin	yes _____	no _____	hands	yes _____	no _____
toes	yes _____	no _____	finger	yes _____	no _____
feet	yes _____	no _____	tongue	yes _____	no _____
skin	yes _____	no _____	ankles	yes _____	no _____ /16

B. Is the child able to tell the function of the following body parts?

nose	yes _____	no _____	hands	yes _____	no _____
ears	yes _____	no _____	teeth	yes _____	no _____
eyes	yes _____	no _____			/5

2. This activity evaluates the child's concepts of print.
    Directions (for worksheet on p. 59)
    Have the child cut apart the words on the solid lines at the top of the page and then paste them in order in the long narrow box under his/her name. Then ask the child to use crayons to illustrate the sentence in the large box.

    A. Did the child paste the words in order from left to right? yes _____ no _____
    B. Are all of the words "right-side-up"? yes _____ no _____
    C. Does the child's picture relate to the sentence? yes _____ no _____

Ask the child to read the sentence pointing to each word as it is being read.

    D. Is the child able to "read" the sentence? yes _____ no _____
       (Remember, reading at this level means has the child memorized the sentence.)
    E. Does the child match the spoken word to the written word while reading and pointing? yes _____ no _____ /5

From *Read It Again! Pre–K*, published by GoodYearBooks. Copyright © 1992 Libby Miller and Liz Rothlein.

hand	is	my	.	Here

Name _____ Date _____

From *Read It Again! Pre-K*, published by GoodYearBooks. Copyright © 1992 Libby Miller and Liz Rothlein.

Additional Activities

1 Phonics: Class "H" Sound Book

Make a class "h" sound book. Have the children cluster all the words that they can think of that begin with the "h" sound. Write the words on a large piece of paper or on the chalkboard so that the children can refer to them as they work.

Give each child a copy of the worksheet on page 62. Model how to draw a picture in the box provided on the worksheet. Ask the children to draw a picture of something that begins with the "h" sound. Encourage them to use their crayons and to make their picture as big as the space. Demonstrate how to color the picture using controlled strokes. Model how to write the "h" word on the line below the picture using a pencil.

Put the completed pages into a class book for everyone to enjoy.

2 Handprint Mural

Make a classroom mural of the children's handprints. Lay out a large sheet of paper on the floor. Then set up Styrofoam meat trays, each containing a thin layer of various colors of tempera paint. Write the caption, HERE ARE MY HANDS, across the top of the paper.

Tell the children to open their hand and press it into one color of paint and then make their handprint on the mural paper. Have each child write his/her name below the handprint. Display the handprints on a bulletin board or wall.

3 Plaster-of-Paris Handprints

Have each child bring in a tinfoil pie plate. Purchase a bag of Plaster of Paris at a hardware store. Mix the Plaster of Paris according to the directions on the package. Pour approximately 3/4" plaster into each pie plate. Help each child put his/her hand into the plaster to make a handprint. Allow the prints to dry overnight. When the plaster is completely dry, remove the pie plate. The handprint can be taken home as a gift.

4 Mr. Five Senses Book

There is nothing a child enjoys more than to have his/her very own book to take home and share with friends, parents, and grandparents. The Mr. Five Senses Book is a delightful way to help children

From *Read It Again! Pre–K*, published by GoodYearBooks. Copyright © 1992 Libby Miller and Liz Rothlein.

become aware of the five senses, the days of the week, and numerals and sets through 5. The sentences on each page follow a definite rhythmic, predictable language pattern that makes beginning reading exciting and fun.

Materials: One copy of Mr. Five Senses (pp. 63–68) for each child, crayons or markers, and a pencil.

First, pose the question, What do you think Mr. Five Senses smelled on Monday? Next, cluster the children's answers on the board. Pass out the worksheet on the sense of smell. Read the sentence on the worksheet (p. 64) with the children. Point to each word as you read. Have the children draw the *one* thing that Mr. Five Senses smelled on Monday. Model how to draw the picture using the entire space provided on the worksheet. Have the children write the word on the line provided.

Follow the same procedure for the sheets about Tuesday through Friday. After the children decide what two things Mr. Five Senses tasted on Tuesday, have them draw the exact same thing in each box (one thing per box). This is to help them learn to follow directions and understand math concepts.

Once the pages of the book are completed, have the children draw Mr. Five Senses on the cover (p. 63).

From *Read It Again! Pre-K*, published by GoodYearBooks. Copyright © 1992 Libby Miller and Liz Rothlein.

Here are my hands for holding a h_____.

From *Read It Again! Pre–K*, published by GoodYearBooks. Copyright © 1992 Libby Miller and Liz Rothlein.

Mr. Five Senses

From *Read It Again! Pre-K*, published by GoodYearBooks. Copyright © 1992 Libby Miller and Liz Rothlein.

On Monday Mr. Five Senses
smelled 1 _____.

From *Read It Again! Pre–K*, published by GoodYearBooks. Copyright © 1992 Libby Miller and Liz Rothlein.

On Tuesday Mr. Five Senses
tasted 2 _____.

From *Read It Again! Pre-K*, published by GoodYearBooks. Copyright © 1992 Libby Miller and Liz Rothlein.

On Wednesday Mr. Five Senses heard 3 _____.

From *Read It Again! Pre–K*, published by GoodYearBooks. Copyright © 1992 Libby Miller and Liz Rothlein.

On Thursday Mr. Five Senses
saw 4 _____.

From *Read It Again! Pre–K*, published by GoodYearBooks. Copyright © 1992 Libby Miller and Liz Rothlein.

On Friday Mr. Five Senses
touched 5 _____.

From *Read It Again! Pre–K*, published by GoodYearBooks. Copyright © 1992 Libby Miller and Liz Rothlein.

IF YOU GIVE A MOUSE A COOKIE

Author
Laura Joffe Numeroff

Illustrator
Felicia Bond

Publisher
Harper & Row, Publishers, Inc.,
1985

Pages
28

Other Books by Numeroff
We know of no other books.

Summary
A little boy invites a mouse to eat a piece of cookie and that is only the beginning. The friendship between the mouse and the boy develop as the story progresses.

Introduction
At the beginning of the story, a little boy is sitting outdoors reading a book and eating cookies. He offers a mouse a cookie and from there on the mouse wants a glass of milk, a straw, a napkin, and so on. As the story unfolds, the little boy and the mouse become friends. Do you think it was a good idea to offer the mouse a cookie? Why or why not?

Discussion Questions

1   Why do you think the boy offered the mouse a cookie? (answers may vary)

2   What do you think would be a good name for the mouse? A good name for the boy? Explain your choices. (answers may vary)

3   Do you think the mouse and the boy knew each other before the boy gave him the cookie? Why or why not? (answers may vary)

4   What are some other things the mouse might have wanted? (answers may vary)

5   What do you think would have happened next if the story had not ended? (answers may vary)

6   What do you think the boy's mother said when she got home and saw the house? (answers may vary)

From *Read It Again! Pre-K*, published by GoodYearBooks. Copyright © 1992 Libby Miller and Liz Rothlein.

ORAL LANGUAGE ACTIVITY
Directions
Write the following rhyme on a large piece of chart paper or on the chalkboard.

> If you give a mouse a cookie,
> He might want a *hat*.
> If you give a mouse a cookie,
> He might want a *pat*.

The focus of this activity is on rhyming word families. Brainstorm words that rhyme with *at* (cat, hat, mat, rat, bat). As the children share their responses, write and illustrate the words on the chalkboard. Use the words to fill in the blanks in the rhyme below. Choral-read with the children.

> If you give a mouse a cookie,
> He might want a _____.
> If you give a mouse a cookie,
> He might want a _____.

Other rhyming word families may be introduced and used to complete the rhyme above (i.e., *-all, -en, -ill*).

You may wish to make a class book using the worksheet on page 71. Place the children in cooperative pairs. Give each child a worksheet. Ask them to decide on a pair of rhyming words that they will use to fill in the blank on the worksheet and then illustrate. Children may use the cluster as a reference or they may try to come up with their own rhyming words.

From *Read It Again! Pre–K*, published by GoodYearBooks. Copyright © 1992 Libby Miller and Liz Rothlein.

From *Read It Again! Pre–K*, published by GoodYearBooks. Copyright © 1992 Libby Miller and Liz Rothlein.

If you give a mouse a cookie,
He might want a _____.

LEARNING CENTER ACTIVITY
Directions

Place the *Mouse's Sorting Center* activity marker (p. 74) at the learning center.

Copy the picture on this page and page 73. Glue them to a sheet of cardboard, laminate it, and cut them apart on the solid lines. Put the picture pieces in a small box. Provide two additional boxes for sorting the pictures. Cover one box with *red* paper and write, "Things mouse *did not* ask for." Cover the other box with *blue* paper and write, "Things mouse *did* ask for." Then ask the children to recall all the things that the mouse asked for after the boy gave him the cookie. Sort the pictures accordingly.

Note: You can make an answer key by copying the pictures on this page and the next, and then color coding them. Draw a *blue* circle around the pictures showing what the *mouse* asked for and a *red* circle around the pictures showing what the mouse *did not ask for.*

From *Read It Again! Pre–K,* published by GoodYearBooks. Copyright © 1992 Libby Miller and Liz Rothlein.

From *Read It Again! Pre–K*, published by GoodYearBooks. Copyright © 1992 Libby Miller and Liz Rothlein.

Mouse's Sorting Center

Things the mouse **asked** for.

Things the mouse **did not ask** for.

From *Read It Again! Pre–K*, published by GoodYearBooks. Copyright © 1992 Libby Miller and Liz Rothlein.

PARENT BULLETIN/HOMEWORK

Name _____ Date _____

This week we are reading *If You Give a Mouse a Cookie* by Laura Joffe Numeroff. It is about a little boy who gave a mouse a cookie, and they become friends. As a class, we would like to have a cookie party and make a cookbook of favorite cookie recipes. This activity will also help the children become familiar with the vocabulary used in recipes and cooking. Please help your child complete the following activities, and please use the following words with your child as you do this week's homework: *recipe, ingredients, directions, stirring, measuring, temperature, oven, bowl, aisle.*

Monday: Sit down with your child and look through a cookbook to choose a favorite cookie recipe. Discuss what a *recipe* is, what *ingredients* you will need, and the *directions* you will have to follow. Make a list of the ingredients you will need, and take it to the store with you on Tuesday.

Tuesday: Take your child to the grocery store to buy the ingredients for your cookies. Have your child discover where the different items are located (i.e., butter in the dairy aisle, flour in the baking aisle).

Wednesday: Please print the recipe in the space provided on the attached sheet. Have your child draw a picture of the ingredients that were needed to make the cookies. We will put all the recipes together into a "Mouse's Favorite Cookie Recipe Book," which will be duplicated and sent home.

Thursday: Have your child help you make a small batch of cookies to send to school on Friday. Allow your child to help measure, stir, and so on.

Friday: Have your child bring his/her cookies and recipe to school to share.

From *Read It Again! Pre–K*, published by GoodYearBooks. Copyright © 1992 Libby Miller and Liz Rothlein.

Box 1:   Write the name of the recipe.

Box 2:   Child: Draw pictures of the ingredients you will need to make the cookies.

Box 3:   Parent: Print the recipe for the cookies.

Shared by _____

From *Read It Again! Pre–K*, published by GoodYearBooks. Copyright © 1992 Libby Miller and Liz Rothlein.

EVALUATION

Name _____ Date _____

1. Provide each child with a sheet of paper that has been folded into eight squares. Have the child draw the eight different things (one per box) that the mouse wanted after the boy gave him a cookie.

2. This activity evaluates the child's concept of print.
   Directions (for worksheet on p. 78)
   Have the child cut apart the words on the solid lines at the top of the page and then paste them in order in the long narrow box under his/her name. Ask the child to illustrate the sentence in the large box.

   A. Did the child paste the words in order from left to right? yes____ no____
   B. Are all the words "right-side-up"? yes____ no____
   C. Is the child able to "read" the sentence? yes____ no____
      (Remember, reading at this level means has the child memorized the sentence.)
   D. Does the child match the spoken word to the written word while reading and pointing? yes____ no____
   E. Does the child's picture relate to the sentence? yes____ no____

From *Read It Again! Pre-K*, published by GoodYearBooks. Copyright © 1992 Libby Miller and Liz Rothlein.

| give | mouse | you | cookie | a | If | a |

Name _____ Date _____

From *Read It Again! Pre–K*, published by GoodYearBooks. Copyright © 1992 Libby Miller and Liz Rothlein.

IF YOU GIVE A
MOUSE A
COOKIE

Additional Activities

1

Mouse Cookies

prepackaged refrigerator sugar cookie mix
wax paper
raisins
toothpicks

Give each child a "lump" of cookie mix. Break off a large piece of the cookie dough to make the mouse's head and two small pieces to form the ears. Roll the large piece into a ball on a piece of wax paper and then flatten (for the head). Roll the two smaller pieces into balls and add ears. Use raisins for the eyes and nose. Use toothpicks to draw whiskers. Place in oven using the temperature guide on the package. Enjoy.

2 What More Could a Mouse Want?

Materials: An 8-1/2" × 11" sheet of paper for each child and a wide variety of magazines.

Ask the children to make a collage of pictures of things the mouse might have wanted if the story had continued. Allow time to share the completed collage.

3 Toy Mice

Toy mice come in many shapes and forms: Mickey Mouse, Minnie Mouse, windup mice, rubber mice. Invite the children to bring in their stuffed or toy mice. Provide a table to display them. Allow time to share.

4 More Mice

Mice are frequently used as characters in books. Ask the children to share other stories that they have read or heard in which a mouse is a character. Invite them to bring in copies of these books; check some out of the library and make them available to the children.

5 Mouse Bookmarks

Materials: grey or brown construction paper, scissors, glue, strips of cardboard cut into bookmark size (2" × 6"), markers or crayons, yarn, hole punch

Have the children cut a circle for the mouse's head and two smaller circles for the ears. Glue these onto the strip of cardboard. Add eyes and a nose using markers or crayons. Glue small strips of yarn for the whiskers. Punch a hole on the bottom end of the cardboard and add a 4" or 5" piece of yarn for the mouse's tail. When the bookmark is used, the head will peek over the top edge of the book and the tail will hang down below the book.

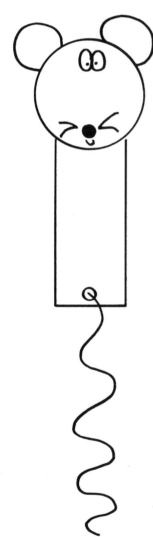

From *Read It Again! Pre–K*, published by GoodYearBooks. Copyright © 1992 Libby Miller and Liz Rothlein.

WHERE'S SPOT?

Author and Illustrator
Eric Hill

Publisher
G. P. Putman's Sons, 1980

Pages
22

Other Books by Hill
Spot's First Easter, Spot Goes to the Farm, Spot Goes to the Beach, Spot Goes to School, Spot's First Christmas, Spot's Birthday Party, Spot's First Walk

Summary
Sally peeks into a closet, a clock, a piano, and so on, as she looks for Spot. While looking for Spot, she finds a bear, a lion, a snake, an alligator, and other animals. Finally, she finds Spot hiding in a basket.

Introduction
The title of this book is *Where's Spot?* Who do you think Spot is? Do you think this is a good title for the book? Why or why not?

Discussion Questions

1 What is the dog's name that is looking for Spot? (Sally) How would you know? (Sally is written on the dog's dish beside Spot's dish)

2 What were some of the animals Sally found while she was looking for Spot? (answers may vary but may include a bear, a monkey, a snake, a hippo, a lion, an alligator, penguins, a turtle)

3 Which animal had the best hiding place? Why? (answers may vary)

4 Who told Sally where to find Spot? (the turtle)

5 If you were looking for a little dog that was hidden in your house, where might you look? (answers may vary)

6 Who do you think Sally is? Explain. (answers may vary)

From *Read It Again! Pre-K*, published by GoodYearBooks. Copyright © 1992 Libby Miller and Liz Rothlein.

ORAL LANGUAGE ACTIVITY
Directions
Sing the following song to the tune of "Oh, Where? Oh, Where Has My Little Dog Gone?"

Oh, where?
Oh, where has my little Spot gone?
Oh, where?
Oh, where can he be?

He is hiding under the big blue chair.

Oh, that's where my little Spot is!

Cluster additional places where Spot might hide. Include a preposition, two adjectives, and a noun. Write a new sentence using the words from the list.

He is hiding _____ the _____ .

| Preposition | Adjectives | | Noun |
	Size	Color	
under	big	red	bed
over	enormous	green	tree
behind	tiny	blue	bird
on	long	purple	boat

Use picture clues to help the children identify the words that were clustered.

Sing the song through and substitute the new sentence for the sentence in the bold type. The new sentences may be written on large pieces of paper, illustrated by the children, and bound into a class book.

From *Read It Again! Pre–K*, published by GoodYearBooks. Copyright © 1992 Libby Miller and Liz Rothlein.

LEARNING ACTIVITY SHEET
Making Predictions

Name _____ Date _____

Directions
Read *Where's Spot?* to the children, stopping before the last page of the story. Ask the children to predict who or what Spot is. Cluster their answers on the chalkboard or on a large piece of chart paper.

In the box on page 83, have the children illustrate what they think Spot would look like. Complete the sentence at the bottom of the page. Share and display the pictures.

From *Read It Again! Pre–K*, published by GoodYearBooks. Copyright © 1992 Libby Miller and Liz Rothlein.

Spot is a _____.

From *Read It Again! Pre-K*, published by GoodYearBooks. Copyright © 1992 Libby Miller and Liz Rothlein.

LEARNING CENTER ACTIVITY
How Big Are Spot's Bones? - Classification
Place the center activity marker (p. 85) at the learning center.

Materials
A permanent marker, paper plates (or plastic containers) to represent dog food bowls, 3 different size dog biscuits, and a large dog biscuit box to store the dog biscuits.

Directions
Label paper plates or plastic containers using the word cards below.

Have the children sort or classify the dog biscuits according to size by placing the biscuits on the right plate or in the appropriate container.

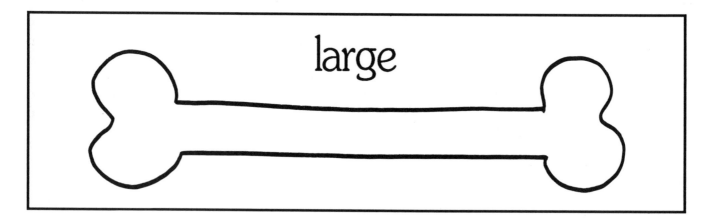

large

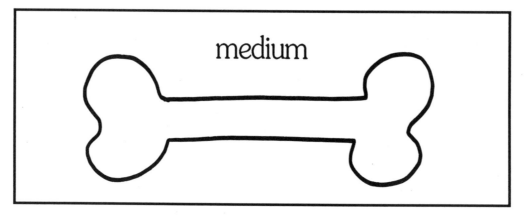

medium

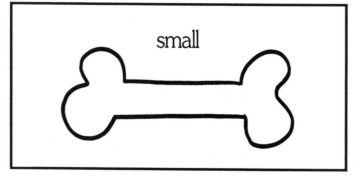

small

From *Read It Again! Pre–K*, published by GoodYearBooks. Copyright © 1992 Libby Miller and Liz Rothlein.

How big are Spot's bones?

From *Read It Again! Pre–K*, published by GoodYearBooks. Copyright © 1992 Libby Miller and Liz Rothlein.

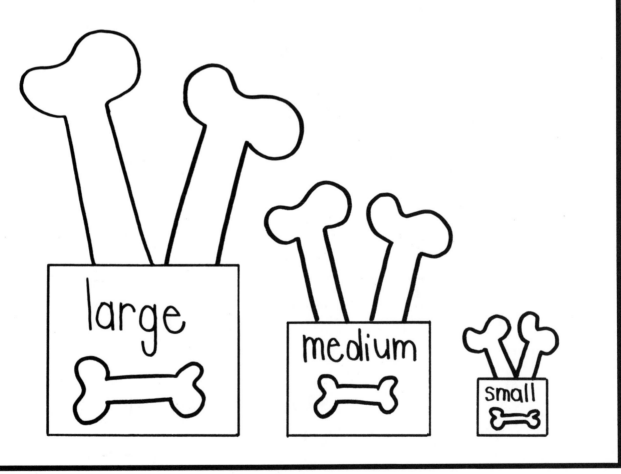

PARENT BULLETIN/HOMEWORK

Name _____ Date _____

This week we are reading *Where's Spot?* by Eric Hill. In this book a dog named Sally is looking for another dog named Spot. She looks behind a door, inside a clock, inside a piano, and under the stairs for Spot and finally finds him in a basket.

    This week's homework will reinforce the positional words that were found in the story: *in, under,* and *behind.*

Monday: Color the picture of Spot below, cut him out, and glue him to a piece of cardboard (the front or back of a cereal box would work well). Next, staple or tape Spot to a popsicle stick or tongue depressor to make a puppet.

Tuesday: Play "Simon Says" by substituting Sally for Simon (i.e., Sally says, "Put Spot in the drawer"). Give oral directions to your child and have him/her hide Spot *in* different places in your home.

Wednesday: Play "Sally Says," and have your child put Spot *under* objects.

Thursday: Continue with "Sally Says" by having your child hide Spot *behind* objects.

Friday: Have your child bring Spot to school.

Parent's Signature _____

From *Read It Again! Pre-K,* published by GoodYearBooks. Copyright © 1992 Libby Miller and Liz Rothlein.

From *Read It Again! Pre-K*, published by GoodYearBooks. Copyright © 1992 Libby Miller and Liz Rothlein.

EVALUATION

Name _____ Date _____

1. Is the child able to identify who Spot is? yes _____ no _____
2. Is the child able to tell where Sally found Spot? yes _____ no _____
3. Have the child point to the picture that shows Spot *under* the hat. Is the child able to point to the picture? yes _____ no _____

4. Have the child point to the picture that shows Spot *in* the wagon. Is the child able to point to the picture? yes _____ no _____

5. Have the child point to the picture that shows Spot *behind* the tree. Is the child able to point to the picture? yes _____ no _____

Additional Activities

1 *Where's Spot?* **Class Book**

Materials: One 4" × 6" and 9" × 12" piece of manila paper for each student, stapler, and crayons.

Brainstorm other places Spot might hide. Record the answers on a large piece of paper or on the chalkboard. (Answers may need illustrations.)

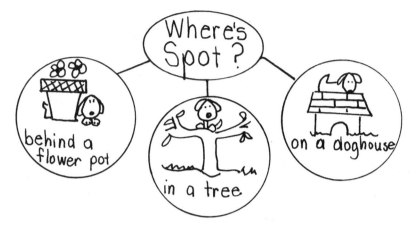

After brainstorming, distribute a 4" × 6" sheet of paper to each child. Ask the child to use the chart or think of an additional place where Spot might hide and illustrate that place on the paper.

Next, staple the picture to the 9" × 12" piece of paper so that you make a flap that can be lifted. Then ask the children to draw a picture of Spot under the flap.

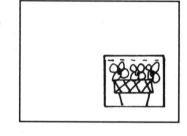

Finally have each child draw his/her picture looking for Spot. Add a speech bubble that says, "Where's Spot?"

From *Read It Again! Pre-K*, published by GoodYearBooks. Copyright © 1992 Libby Miller and Liz Rothlein.

From *Read It Again! Pre-K*, published by GoodYearBooks. Copyright © 1992 Libby Miller and Liz Rothlein.

2 Phonics: Class "S" Sound Book

Materials: One 12" round paper circle for each child (a 45 rpm record makes a good pattern for a circle), one 9" × 12" piece of heavy paper (tagboard, posterboard), stapler, crayons, wiggle eyes (optional).

Make a class sound book by having the children cluster all the words they can think of that begin with the "s" sound (as in *sun*). Write the words on the chalkboard so that the children can refer to them as they work. Additional "s" words: star, soap, sunflower, skin, Santa, Superman, sick, sand, suit, suitcase, socks, silver, slipper, Spot, Sally, sea, snow, snowman, soup, sun, sunbeam.

Give each child a circle. Have the children select *one* "s" word to illustrate on their circle for the class book. Write along the bottom edge of the circle, "Spot sees _____." Fill in the blank with the word that corresponds to the picture that the child has drawn. Collect the finished pictures and follow the directions below to put the book together.

Add a plain circle to be used for the cover and Spot's face. Staple to the top of the poster board.

Use markers or construction paper to add ears, eyes, and nose.

Add body.

3 Where Is Spot Hiding? Class Game

Bring in a stuffed dog (or have a child loan a stuffed dog to the class) and name it Spot. Send four or five children out of the room at a time. Allow one of the children remaining in the room to hide Spot. When the children who have been out of the room return, tell them to ask questions about where the dog is hiding—Is Spot in a desk? Is Spot under a desk? The child who hid the dog may respond be saying "you are hot" if the guess was close or "you are cold" if the guess was not close. Continue until the dog is found, or establish a certain number of guesses that are allowed before telling where the dog is hidden.

4 A Trip to the Pet Shop

Take the children on a field trip to a pet store and have them look at all the different kinds of pets, including dogs. If possible, have someone at the pet store tell the children the important things they should know about owning a dog as a pet. If it is not possible to go to a pet store, pet store managers may be interested in bringing some of the pets to the classroom. A dog obedience trainer would also make an interesting guest speaker.

5 Pet Day

Set aside a specific day for pet sharing. When appropriate, some pets may be brought into the classroom for a short time. If this is not appropriate or feasible, ask the children to bring in pictures of their pets. Display these pictures and allow time for the children to share their pets. As a culmination to this activity, list all the different pets that the children have. Make tally marks beside each pet to find the number of children who have each of the pets mentioned.

Make a graph on the chalkboard or on a large sheet of paper showing the different pets the children have.

6 Hot Dog Kabobs

Try these delicious "Hot Dog Kabobs" for snacktime.

Hot Dog Kabobs

1/2 hot dog per child	cherry tomatoes
wooden skewers	green pepper chunks
pineapple chunks	mushrooms

Cut the hot dogs into 1/2" pieces. Show the children how to put the items on the skewer by alternating the foods. Finally, put them on a broiler pan and bake at 375° for about 15 minutes. Serve on paper plates.

From *Read It Again! Pre-K*, published by GoodYearBooks. Copyright © 1992 Libby Miller and Liz Rothlein.

WHOSE MOUSE ARE YOU?

Author
Robert Kraus

Illustrator
Jose Aruego

Publisher
Macmillan Publishing Co., Inc.,
1970

Pages
28

Other Books by Kraus
*The Good Mousekeeper,
Another Mouse to Feed,
Herman the Helper, How
Spider Saved Valentine's Day,
Leo the Late Bloomer, Mert the
Blurt, Milton the Early Riser,
Spider's First Day At School*

Summary
Whose Mouse Are You? tells about a mouse that couldn't find his family. Finally, he rescues the members of his family and gains a new baby brother. At the end, everyone is happy.

Introduction
This is a story about a mouse that felt lonely because his family was not with him. Have you ever been all alone? If so, how did it feel? If not, how do you think it would feel?

Discussion Questions

1 How do you think the mouse felt at the beginning of the story? (sad, lonely) Why? (because the mouse was lonely without a family)

2 Where was the mouse's mother? (inside a cat) Where was the mouse's father? (caught in a trap) Where was the mouse's sister? (far from home) Where was the mouse's brother? (he didn't have one)

3 Do you think the mouse was clever? Explain. (answers may vary)

4 Why do you think the sister was far from home? (answers may vary)

5 Is this story real or pretend? Explain. (answers may vary)

6 How did the mouse feel at the end of the story? (happy) Why? (he had his family back plus a new brother)

From *Read It Again! Pre-K*, published by GoodYearBooks. Copyright © 1992 Libby Miller and Liz Rothlein.

Materials
Pictures of mice including photographs and cartoons, a large piece of chart paper, markers, a sentence strip

Directions
1. Display the pictures of mice. Have the children describe the different characteristics they see (furry, fat, gray, pink, long-tailed, silly, funny, tiny, goofy, dizzy, creepy, sad, happy). Write the words on the board and illustrate their meaning.

2. On the large piece of chart paper, write the following:

   Three _____ mice.
   Three _____ mice.
   See how they run.
   See how they run.
   They all ran after the farmer's wife.
   She cut off their tails with a carving knife.
   Did you ever see such a sight in your life
   As three _____ mice?

   Write the describing words that the children used to characterize the mice on a sentence strip. Insert the words in the space provided to change the nursery rhyme, such as three *silly* mice, three *long-tailed* mice, three *pink* mice.

3. The new verses can be printed on additional pages of chart paper and bound together to make a big book. Children can illustrate the verses using markers or crayons.

From *Read It Again! Pre–K*, published by GoodYearBooks. Copyright © 1992 Libby Miller and Liz Rothlein.

LEARNING CENTER ACTIVITY
Place the *Mouse Costume Center* activity marker (p. 94) at the learning center

Materials
One large brown grocery bag for each child (with a circle cut out for child's face to show through), pipe cleaners (for whiskers), yarn (for tail), hole punch, felt markers or crayons, glue.

Directions
Place supplies needed for the costume at the center. Then model how to make the paper-bag costume. Have the children take turns creating their own mouse costume.

Write the text from *Whose Mouse Are You?* on a large piece of chart paper. Have the children wear their costumes while sitting in a circle and choral-reading *Whose Mouse Are You?* Allow the children time to interact and act out the mouse characters by asking each other the following questions:

Whose mouse are you?
Where is your mother?
Where is your father?
Where is your sister?
Where is your brother?

From *Read It Again! Pre-K*, published by GoodYearBooks. Copyright © 1992 Libby Miller and Liz Rothlein.

Mouse Costume Center

front   back

From *Read It Again! Pre–K*, published by GoodYearBooks. Copyright © 1992 Libby Miller and Liz Rothlein.

PARENT BULLETIN/HOMEWORK

Name _____ Date _____

This week we are reading *Whose Mouse Are You?* by Robert Kraus. This is a story about a mouse that can't find his family. Finally he rescues the members of his family and gains a new brother, and everyone lives happily ever after.

This week's homework will reinforce the following math concepts: recognizing numerals to 5, counting objects to five, making sets to five, and making comparisons.

Monday: Collect the following materials that you will need to complete the homework activities for this week: the mouse pattern, crayons or felt markers, yarn, a hole punch, and cardboard or posterboard.

Using the attached mouse pattern, cut five mice out of cardboard or posterboard. Have your child color the mice, adding eyes and whiskers. Then put one dot on the first mouse, two dots on the second mouse, three dots on the third mouse, and so forth. Punch a hole in each mouse where the tail would be. Cut five pieces of string or yarn of *different* (*or varying*) lengths (i.e., 5", 4", 3"). Insert the yarn or string through the holes and tie it securely to make a tail for each mouse.

Tuesday: Have your child put the mice in order—the longest tail to the shortest tail. Then ask your child which mouse has the shortest tail? Which has the longest tail? Which has the middle-size tail?

Wednesday: Ask your child to count the dots on each mouse and then place them in correct numerical order. After the mice are put in order, have your child count the mice.

From *Read It Again! Pre-K*, published by GoodYearBooks. Copyright © 1992 Libby Miller and Liz Rothlein.

Thursday: You will need five pieces of paper with the numerals 1, 2, 3, 4, and 5 written on them (a different numeral on each piece of paper). Have your child put the five mice in order starting from the left with the mouse with one dot followed by two dots, three dots, and so on. Have your child match the paper with the numerals on it to the mouse with the matching number of dots.

Friday: Review the activities with your child and have him/her bring the mice to school on Monday. We will continue to use the mice at school to reinforce math concepts. Thank you and have fun!!!

From *Read It Again! Pre-K*, published by GoodYearBooks. Copyright © 1992 Libby Miller and Liz Rothlein.

EVALUATION

Name _____ Date _____

1. This activity evaluates the child's ability to recall details from an orally read story.

   Is the child able to answer the following questions?

   A. Where is the mouse's mother? (inside the cat) yes _____ no _____
   B. Where is the mouse's father? (caught in a trap) yes _____ no _____
   C. Where is the mouse's sister? (far from home) yes _____ no _____
   D. What did the mouse get at the end of the story? (a brother) yes _____ no _____

2. This activity evaluates the child's concept of print.
   Directions (for worksheet on p. 98)
   Have the child cut apart the words on the solid lines at the top of the page and then paste them in order in the long narrow box. Ask the child to illustrate the sentence in the large box.

   1. Did the child paste the words in order from left to right? yes _____ no _____
   2. Are all the words "right-side-up"? yes _____ no _____
   3. Is the child able to "read" the sentence? yes _____ no _____
   4. Does the child match the spoken word to the written word while reading and pointing? yes _____ no _____
   5. Does the child's picture relate to the sentence? yes _____ no _____

From *Read It Again! Pre-K*, published by GoodYearBooks. Copyright © 1992 Libby Miller and Liz Rothlein.

| mouse | you | Whose | ? | are |

Name _____ Date _____

From *Read It Again! Pre–K*, published by GoodYearBooks. Copyright © 1992 Libby Miller and Liz Rothlein.

WHOSE
MOUSE ARE
YOU?

Additional Activities

1 Mouse Puppets

Materials: Scissors, construction paper, paste or glue, markers, Styrofoam cups, yarn.

Have the children tear or cut pieces of construction paper to make mouse ears and glue them to the cup. Next they can use markers to draw the eyes, nose, and whiskers. Third, have them punch a hole in the appropriate place on the cup and string a length of yarn through it to make a tail. Finally, have the children dramatize *Whose Mouse Are You?* using their mouse puppets.

2 Mouse Cheese Delights

Discuss a mouse's favorite food—cheese. Using the recipe below, make "Mouse Cheese Delights" and have a party to celebrate the mouse family reunion. In addition to the ingredients listed, you will need an iron, paper plates, and plastic knives.

Mouse Cheese Delights

2 slices of bread for each student
butter, softened
2 slices of cheese for each student
tinfoil

Help children create their own grilled cheese sandwiches. Each child will need to butter the outside of each slice of bread (make sure the butter is soft enough to spread easily). Next, have them place slices of cheese on the bread. Wrap the sandwich in tinfoil. Then using an iron, iron both sides of the tinfoil (1 to 2 minutes on each side). Unwrap, eat, and enjoy!

---

3 Different Kinds of Mice

There are many books about mice. Make available books such as *Once a Mouse* by Marcia Brown and *Alexander and the Wind-Up Mouse* by Leo Lionni. Read the books aloud or allow the children to peruse them. Then discuss which mouse stories they like best and why. The differences and similarities can also be discussed.

4 Mice Pets

Mice make good classroom pets. Contact your local pet store and investigate the possibility of getting mice for your classroom—if not on a permanent basis, perhaps for a day or two. Allow the children to observe the mice. Finally, discuss the characteristics of the mice they observe.

5 A Mouse Tail

Cut ribbon or crepe paper into approximately 3-ft. lengths to create a tail for each child. Attach "tails" to each child's back using tape or tucking them into pants or skirts. Encourage the children to move like mice, swishing their tails about, as music is played.

From *Read It Again! Pre-K,* published by GoodYearBooks. Copyright © 1992 Libby Miller and Liz Rothlein.

6 "Quiet as a Mouse" Award

Create a "Quiet as a Mouse" award by making a simple mouse shape and writing "Quiet as a Mouse" on it. Then explain to children that mice move very quietly. Explain that the phrase "quiet as a mouse" is a saying that has been passed down over the years to mean someone who is very quiet. Tell them that if they are very quiet for a specified period or during a specific activity where quiet is needed, they will receive the "Quiet as a Mouse" award to wear.

7 Thumbprint Mice

Provide an inked stamp pad and some small sheets of paper. Show the children how they can make thumbprints by putting their thumbs on the stamp pad and then the sheet of paper. Once the prints are made, have the children create a mouse by adding ears, whiskers, eyes, and a tail using a thin felt-tip marker. Encourage them to make the mouse family they read about in *Whose Mouse Are You?*

WESTFIELD PUBLIC LIBRARY
333 West Hoover Street
Westfield, IN 46074